Beyond Skepticism
All the Way to Enlightenment

Also by
Stephen Hawley Martin:

The Seach for Nina Fletcher

Out of Body, Into Mind

Beyond Skepticism
All The Way to Enlightenment

by

Stephen Hawley Martin

The Oaklea Press
Richmond, Virginia

FIRST EDITION
First Printing, 1995

Preliminary Library of Congress Cataloging-in-Publication Data

Martin, Stephen Hawley, 1944-
    Beyond Skepticism: All the Way to Enlightenment /
Stephen Hawley Martin

Bibliography, Index

ISBN 0-9646601-4-8

1. Metaphysics 2. Spirituality 3. Self-Actualization (psychology) 4. Reincarnation
I. Title.

1 2 3 4 5 6 7 8 9 0

Contents

Here (in this experience) all blades of grass, wood, and stone, all things are One . . . when is a man in mere understanding? When he sees one thing separated from another. And when is he above mere understanding? When he sees all in all, then a man stands above mere understanding.

Meister Eckhart (1260-1327)

Introduction: Who This Book is for and Its Objective

Whether or not you recognize it, all humanity is on a spiritual journey. Indeed, as you will see if you continue to read, this unfolding is part of the underlying reason for life on earth. An image of this procession comes from W. E. (Ernest) Butler, the founder of the Ibis Fraternity, an organization dedicated to helping and teaching others on the path. He likened the spiritual evolution of mankind to a great crowd making its way along a road that winds up a hill,[1] plodding forward as a flock of sheep might, kicking up dust but moving slowly, stopping now and then, scrapping and biting each other; now and then getting panicky and shifting one way or the other; often hardly moving ahead at all. With this in mind, let me ask whether you have made the decision to break out of the pack. The road can be difficult, especially when all you can see is a cloud of dust in the rearview mirror. It can be lonely out in front, but if you are a seeker of Truth, you haven't much choice in the matter. You must proceed regardless of the consequences. This book was written for you.

In *Further Along The Road Less Traveled* Scott Peck discusses his theory of the stages of spiritual growth.[2] In the interest of explaining what I mean by being "out in front" I will briefly describe them for you, although you may wish to read about them firsthand and in more detail in the original work.

Stage One is the Chaotic/Antisocial. People at this level are unprincipled and antisocial. In effect, Stage One is a condition totally absent of spirituality. While they may pretend to be loving, all of their relationships are self-serving and manipulative. Truly, they are looking out for number one. Being unprincipled, they have nothing to govern themselves except their own wills, which is why people in this stage are often found in trouble or difficulty, in jail, in hospitals or out on the street sleeping on steam vents. Peck points out that it is possible for them to to be self-disciplined from time to time and in the service of their ambition to rise to positions of prestige and power.[3] Some evangelistic preachers and politicians come to mind. I was once acquainted with someone I now recognize as a Stage One individual who headed a successful company. Under his direction the firm became one of the fastest growing in its field. The man was a brilliant speaker and strategist. He had a photographic memory. But he was without principles, scruples or anything close to what we might call a conscience. Even though he was married he took pride in himself as a master of seduction of members of the opposite sex. Figuratively speaking, he left the landscape strewn with the bodies of his lovers and adversaries and to my knowledge never felt an inkling of remorse. This man was extremely successful for a time and made millions before the age of forty. But in the end his closest colleagues turned on and ousted him, perhaps because they feared they too would someday become victims of his egocentric nature.

The Stage One person has a difficult time of it if he ever happens to get in touch with himself and realize the chaos within and the hurt he has caused. It seems possible some unexplained suicides may have come about as a result.

Or a happier possibility is that the Stage One personality may suddenly and dramatically convert to Stage Two, which has been labeled the Formal/Institutional. Those in it depend on an institution to keep them on the straight and narrow. This may be a prison, the military, or a rigidly organized corporation. But for most in our society it is the church.

Stage Two individuals tend to be attached to ritual and dogma and become very upset if someone challenges it or tries to institute change. We all know of those who take the Bible literally, who believe the world was created in six twenty-four hour days and that man was brought into being as a fully-evolved *Homo sapiens* known as Adam. Rather than seeing the story as a myth recounting the period in the ascent of man when we evolved from creatures driven by instinct into self-conscious human beings, these usually well-meaning folk believe that God literally banished the very first man (whose name was Adam) and the very first woman (whose name was Eve) from a real place known as the Garden of Eden.

Stage Two people think of God as an external being and almost always envision Him as up there on a cloud looking down, making a list and checking it twice. More than likely they picture a man who looks remarkably like Michelangelo's depiction on the ceiling of the Sistine Chapel, and they ascribe to him the power and the will to make them extremely sorry for their transgressions. To quote Scott Peck, God is seen as "a giant benevolent cop in the sky."[4]

I want to state clearly, however, that many Christians and followers of other religions are by no means stuck in Stage Two. I personally know many who are well into Stage Four. A characteristic these more advanced believers share is an image of God as immanent in all of creation.

Before we look at this, let's consider the characteristics of Stage Three. It's not surprising that these folks are likely to have been raised in a family headed by Stage Two parents (whether Christian, Buddhist, Jewish or Muslim) and as a result internalized their parents' religious and moral principles. By the time they reached adolescence, however, they were questioning the dogma ("I looked at

Playboy and God didn't strike me blind. Who needs these silly myths and superstitions?"). To the horror of their parents they eventually fell away from the church and became doubters or agnostics or atheists. This is the Skeptic/Individual stage. Its members are not religious but neither are they antisocial. They are often deeply involved in social or ecological causes. Frequently they are scientists and almost always are scientific-minded. To my way of thinking they comprise a plurality of the educated middle and upper middle class in America and can be found in large numbers teaching our children and young adults in schools and universities. The media are chock full of them. They are reporters, columnists and commentators. Because they frequently rigidly adhere to mechanistic views of reality and to secular humanist philosophy they often seem to Stage Two and Four individuals to be misguided. They usually are unwilling to consider the existence of anything they cannot see or touch. Scott Peck believes, however, that they do tend to be truth seekers and if they seek truth deeply enough and widely enough and get enough bits and pieces to catch glimpses of the big picture they will come to an understanding that the truth curiously resembles the primitive myths and superstitions held so dear by their Stage Two parents. It is at the point of catching these glimpses that Stage Three individuals begin to convert to Stage Four, which has been called the Mystical/Communal.

Stage Four individuals are referred to as mystical because they see a kind of cohesion behind physical reality. As Dr. Peck puts it, "Seeing that kind of interconnectedness beneath the surface, mystics of all cultures and religions have always spoken in terms of unity and community."[5]

The nature of this cohesion and the implications of it will be dealt with at length as we go forward. If you deny its possibility, if you have not had at least one small fleeting glimpse of it, then you have not arrived at the threshold of Stage Four and in all likelihood are not ready for what I have to say. In fact you may even be antagonized by it.

How can this be? We tend to be threatened by those in the stages of spiritual development ahead of us and by what they believe. For example, while people in Stage One may seem as though nothing bothers them, underneath they are terrified of virtually everyone, which explains why my Stage One acquaintance left so many bloody bodies in his path. Stage Two folks see Stage One as fertile ground for conversions, however, recognizing them to be sinners who need to be shown the light. Conversely, they tend to be threatened by Stage Three skeptics and are even more put off by Stage Four mystical types who seem to believe the same things but with a kind of freedom they find terrifying.

Moving up the ladder, Stage Threes certainly aren't threatened by Stage Ones, except when they find themselves facing one with a gun or a knife, and they see Stage Twos as mostly idiotic zealots, harmless except for their efforts to put prayer back in the schools and to outlaw abortion. But they are threatened by Stage Fours who seem to be scientifically minded but also inexplicably believe in this crazy God thing. Scott Peck says, "If you mentioned the word 'conversion' to the Stage Three people, they would see a vision of a missionary arm-twisting a heathen and they would go through the roof."[6]

Regardless of the skepticism of Stage Three individuals, mystics and spiritual thinkers throughout the centuries and in all societies have believed in the connectedness sensed by Stage Four individuals. In her best-selling book, *A History of God,* Karen Armstrong writes, "One of the reasons why religion seems irrelevant today is that many of us no longer have the sense that we are surrounded by the unseen. Our scientific culture educates us to focus our attention on the physical and material world in front of us. This method of looking at the world has achieved great results. One of its consequences, however, is that we have, as it were, edited out the sense of the 'spiritual' or the 'holy' which pervades the lives of people in more traditional societies at every level and which was once an essential component of our human experience of the world."[7] Indeed, in the television series *Power of Myth*, Joseph Campbell said that the basic theme of all mythology is the existence of an invisible plane which supports the visible.[8]   As we shall see, without this unseen world nothing in the physical dimension would be possible.

The objective of this book is to explore the nature of the invisible and in so doing determine how it affects you and me. We will ask and answer how we came to be in this physical realm and the reason we are here. If you read attentively and allow yourself to suspend disbelief as you do, you will find that you can use the insights which come to spur yourself forward on your journey toward full awakening and empowerment.

My purpose is not to twist your arm or in any way try to convert you to my way of thinking. It is to unveil the invisible world and man's purpose in a way that those moving away from skepticism will understand and can accept and to share with them techniques which have helped me get in touch and stay in touch with my higher self. By doing so I've arrived on a path that promises a more fulfilling life than I ever imagined possible.

As you read bear in mind that at the human level all truth is relative, which means that even though you make an effort to read with an open mind you may not be able to accept all that is said. Our world view changes as we grow. You may wish to reread this book later. You may gain new insights and perhaps be ready to accept truths that had eluded you.   For now, disregard what seems off base or far-fetched. All we need to agree on is that a plane exists that is somehow behind or underlying physical reality and that this plane cannot be detected by the ordinary senses. If you have ever had even a fleeting glimpse of the cohesion it creates, if you sincerely want to understand and visualize it in a way few people do, if you want your thinking and imagination stimulated about the implications of this plane both to you personally and for mankind in general, then by all means proceed.

May what lies ahead deepen your conviction and carry you to new heights. May you achieve your own personal enlightenment.

Beyond Skepticism

Chapter One: A New Vision of the Invisible

Most Boomers probably were born into Stage Two families, which is likely why they grew up confident enough to rebel, but my parents already were firmly entrenched in Stage Three when I arrived on the scene. This didn't mean I got to skip Stage Three. (We don't skip stages.) Skeptics like my parents are susceptible to their own brand of dogma: Materialism. This is what I was handed to rebel against. I had to become skeptical about their beliefs before I could move to Stage Four. I now realize that this was part of the plan for me from the beginning, although I don't recall ever having a particular urge to rebel. No one ever said I couldn't look at *Playboy.*

How did someone in my situation get past the idea held from childhood that the universe is constructed of separate, distinct, unconnected pieces? How does one do that if one was brought up as I was by parents who told me that if I wanted to fool around with my girlfriend, be sure to take all the necessary precautions?

Oh, they weren't amoral. We went to church. It was one that nowadays I might thoroughly enjoy, a Unitarian Church founded by Thomas Jefferson or so I was told. Unitarians bring people together into one congregation regardless of their specific beliefs so you won't find one where the preacher or anyone else comes at you waving some dogma or other. No doubt this appealed to my parents. In those days the Sunday sermons at this one were thinly veiled lectures on psychology or philosophy.

In my household the universe was pictured as a giant clock constructed by the Creator and the unalterable laws of physics were built into the mechanism. This clock had been set loose and required and received no further help or interference from God. At least that's what my parents believed. They couldn't abide Bible thumpers. My mother once yanked me out of a church-run kindergarten after I told her the teacher had read us the story of Noah and the flood.

Then came high school and college where Newton's mechanical view of things was not only reinforced but taught as unquestioned fact. Instead of a clock, however, it was a giant billiard game. Instead of God creating it and building the laws into it, the universe just happened. It was caused by a Big Bang. The laws were laws, nothing more; fundamental to the basic structure. (Looking back I realize the laws of physics replaced God.)

Somehow this didn't sit well. What was here before God or the Bang or the laws? How had life come about? Was it really possible for something as complex as a DNA molecule to form by accident? And what then? It became a writhing mass of protoplasm when lightning struck? Then tiny one-celled animals had evolved by random chance into all the elaborate forms of life on the planet today?

If so, how had the first kidney evolved? The first liver? The eye? Gills? Lungs? Was it possible that enough monkeys with enough typewriters could actually write *War and Peace?*

With no typos?

What I did not know then was that a new religion had grown up from the time of Newton and Descartes called Materialism. This is what my parents and teachers believed in, and it has as its primary tenet that only matter is real. Even human consciousness can be explained in terms of matter.[1]   What the professors didn't say is that a great deal cannot be explained within its confines. For example, how do different cells know their role is to become a kidney or a foot or a brain when an animal or human embryo grows in the womb? The professor of biology said the information is encoded in the genes, but that may not be true. It hasn't been demonstrated. The genes dictate the primary structure of proteins, not the individual parts of the body. Given the right genes and hence the right proteins, and the right systems by which protein synthesis is controlled, an organism is supposed to assemble itself. But how? As the Cambridge-educated biochemist Rupert Sheldrake wrote, "This is rather like delivering the right materials to a building site at the right times and expecting a house to grow spontaneously."[2]

We will return to this. The point is, believing dogmatically in Materialism takes as much faith as believing Adam literally was created by God out of dirt and came into the world as a fully-evolved *Homo sapiens.* Now there is something to rebel against.

I don't recall precisely when I first began to doubt. Perhaps it began with my penchant for waking up before the alarm clock went off. On a day I had an important meeting or a plane to catch at say 6:30 in the morning, I'd wake up just seconds before the alarm. My eyes would pop open and my hand would go out and push down the plunger an instant before the second hand reached twelve and the buzzer sounded.   Not so extraordinary, perhaps, and easily explained from a Materialistic point of view. My body, like everyone else's body is equipped with its own biological clock. At least that's the explanation I received. No one could say where the clock was located, but it must have been there. Otherwise how could this happen?

I did wonder, though, how my biological clock could adjust so quickly to different time zones or to a clock in a hotel room which was a few minutes fast or slow. It also struck me as odd when the phenomenon continued in Europe and I was six time zones away from home.

Another thing that troubled me was a feeling I often get when I walk into a room or step onto an elevator and someone is watching me. I turn. They look away.

How could I know?

Then one day I went to a luncheon given by a television station and there was a door prize, a new Sony Trinitron. When the time came for the drawing I pulled my ticket from the pocket of my trousers, looked at it and experienced a sensation which said I was going to win.

The numbers were read and all of them matched.

How was this possible?

Coincidence was the likely explanation, I told myself, although this didn't seem adequate. How could coincidence explain a feeling?

I remained a faithful Materialist to the outside world because I didn't want to be excommunicated, but on the sly I was now on the lookout for more inexplicable incidents. The next one came at the end of a vacation in Corsica where my wife and my three-year-old daughter and I spent a week at the summer home of one of my wife's childhood friends.

Both my wife and her friend were French, or more accurately the friend was half French and half Corsican. No matter what this mixture might be called, this young woman was most definitely not a Materialist. I suspect it is often the case with those who feel particularly close to a place as Corsicans do to their "Isle of Beauty." I found myself amused by what I considered to be her fantasies of spooks and fairies lurking here and there in the four-o'clocks or in mountain glades and her believing she could tell fortunes using tea leaves and tarot cards.

I resisted her attempts to tell mine until the last night of our visit. Even then, I limited my participation to only two cards which I pulled from the deck and handed back to her.

"You are going on a journey," she told me. "On this journey you will assist a young man who is blond and in need of your help."

She was half right, I thought. I was going on a journey. (We were leaving the next morning.) But that didn't prove anything because she knew it as well as I. As for a blond young man, well, I forgot about it until I landed in Marseille and was standing in line at the airport bank to change a few hundred dollars into francs.

The young man in front reached the window, unfolded an enormous bill and handed it to the teller who looked at it and muttered, "Ooh, la, la." What followed was an animated exchange where neither party had the slightest idea what the other was saying, the bank teller speaking French and shaking his head and the young man, whom I now saw was as blond as Marilyn Monroe except his hair was thinning on top, speaking English with a Nordic accent and growing more and more desperate by the second. As it turned out he was Norwegian, had just stepped off the plane from Oslo and the bill was koner. Fortunately I knew enough French to understand the teller was trying to explain to him that he'd have to go to the main office of the bank in downtown Marseille to change it. Otherwise, the poor fellow might have spent the day arguing (about what he didn't know) and the night wandering around Marseille with a tin cup in his hand. I'd "assisted" him all right, a blond young man as our hostess had predicted.

This "coincidence" got me thinking again, and it wasn't long, only a matter of hours, before I had another one to chew on. It happened that same night.

Marseille is not a stop I'd recommend to someone who has the choice of going somewhere else in the south of France, but even this filthy port city has one or two neighborhoods with charm. Such was the case with one where another of my wife's childhood friends lived. Her home was located beneath the statue of Notre Dame which looks down on the city from atop the highest hill and has a view of the harbor and the island fortress of Count of Monte Cristo fame. Built into the side of a steep hill, the house has three levels, the bottom of which is an English basement at grade with a terrace in front. The friend lived in the big old place with her widowed mother, neither of whom worked outside the home, and I imagine money was in short supply. Perhaps as a result they had turned the ground floor into a separate apartment and rented it out. Lo and behold the first tenant was a dashing young man who worked with Jacques

Cousteau and gallivanted around the world on a converted mine sweeper called the Calypso. Living there as he did when he wasn't gallivanting, he and my wife's friend fell in love and got engaged. The four of us had chummed around before my wife and I were married and when we tied the knot this fellow had been the French equivalent of my best man and she had been the maid of honor.

That was in happier times.

The mood was somber when we arrived at the house in Marseille that year because the dashing young man was dead. Philippe had always had a fascination with death. He sincerely believed it wasn't the end; that we enter another dimension when we "cross over." I believe this preoccupation may have led to his harboring a subconscious death wish. He would barrel down a narrow Marseille city street on a 750cc Triumph motorcycle at 120 miles an hour. (Once he did this with me hanging on the back praying as no Materialist had ever prayed before.) He also flew small planes and skydived, and of course deep sea diving was part of his job. He can still be seen in reruns of Cousteau playing ring around the rosy with sharks.

The sad part of the story is that Philippe had fallen into despair and his death was thought to have been a suicide. Several things had gone wrong. First, by that time (mid-'70s) Cousteau wasn't making trips to exotic locales anymore. Replacing a job as a seafaring adventurer isn't easy. To keep body and soul together he'd taken one as the captain of a boat that tended off shore oil rigs but was bored to death. Second, his romance with my wife's good friend was on the rocks. They had broken up and she refused to see him. Who knows what else might have gone wrong, but whatever, he was found dead in his cabin at sea.

On different occasions Philippe had told close friends including his ex-fiancée that if it were possible to communicate once he crossed over, he would. The fiancée was aflutter when we arrived because her wristwatch had stopped when his funeral had begun and had not resumed functioning until the moment the funeral had ended. I'd had watches start and stop plenty of times so I didn't see that this proved anything, but I kept the thought to myself.

Later that evening, after dinner, I decided to turn in early. It looked as though my wife and her friend were well on the way to staying up all night talking, which they did incessantly in French. Trying to keep up with a conversation in French had always given me a headache so I suggested I put Sophie (my three-year-old) to bed and turn in myself.

I went to find Sophie who was in another room playing with her dolls and the two of us descended a circular staircase and walked hand in hand through a storage room. As we had in years past, we were sleeping in Philippe's old apartment. When I opened the door it immediately struck me that nothing had changed. Every piece of furniture, every wall hanging was exactly as he'd left it, and I experienced the most bizarre sensation he was there among his belongings, somehow permeating everything: the American Indian throw on the bed, the primitive masks and spears on the walls, the little statues and knickknacks he'd brought back from all over the world, many representing local deities or gods of fertility. The feeling of his presence was palpable and it seemed to close in and surround me. But I did not say anything because I did not want to upset my daughter. Instead I got her into her pajamas, went through the usual routine of a bedtime story and put her down in a child's bed which had been placed at the foot of Philippe's.

I crawled under the covers, took a book and tried to read. But I must confess I had difficulty. I felt Philippe's presence stronger than ever, particularly when I looked at a hand-woven wool wall hanging of a sunburst. It reminded me of the rising sun of Japan and my eyes kept being drawn to its circular center.

Then came a small voice: "Don't think about ghosts. It doesn't do any good to think about ghosts."

I'd thought my daughter was asleep but she was sitting up, as was every hair on my body. I didn't know she even knew what a ghost was, or rather what a ghost was supposed to be since ghosts don't exist. Nothing exists except matter, right?

I hoped so.

In retrospect I probably should have asked, "Why do

you say that, dear?" but to tell the truth I wasn't thinking clearly. Instead I said, "That's correct, dear. It doesn't do any good to think about ghosts." She laid down and I didn't hear from her again that night.

Okay, so what caused her to sit up and make that rather interesting observation? It seems to me there are three possibilities:

First, although I don't recall we'd ever talked about it and neither did my wife when I told her of the incident later, Sophie may have been aware that Philippe was dead and that we were spending the night in a dead man's apartment. This unsettling fact may have played on her mind just as it obviously played on mine. In this case she may have been reassuring herself. "There's no need to be afraid of the dark. There aren't really any goblins under the bed." Only, my experience as a father of three is that young children believe there are goblins under the bed no matter how emphatically one assures them they're not. Anyway, she didn't say that ghosts aren't real. She said I ought not to think about them.

Second, she may have picked up on my thoughts through mental telepathy. People who believe in such things think those who are closely related such as a mother and son or father and daughter or sister and brother are particularly susceptible. I was indeed thinking about a ghost. Maybe she tuned in on this and decided to give me a piece of worldly, three-year-old daughter advice. I must say, however, that she refrained from dishing it out again until she was approximately nineteen. (As every parent of a nineteen-year-old can verify, at that age the child knows everything and the parent knows nothing, encumbered as parents are by the stupidity that comes from having reached one's forties.)

The third possibility is that Philippe was using Sophie's three-year-old half-asleep mind to communicate as he'd promised he would. If so the message he chose is particularly significant in light of his former preoccupation with death and his reported suicide. "Don't think about ghosts. It doesn't do any good." I've taken that to mean, live life because death will come soon enough.

Maybe you can think of another explanation. If so,

22

write to me care of the publisher of this book because I'd be interested in hearing it. Otherwise, take your pick from the possibilities listed above. Be advised, though, that the second two require something to have happened which Materialists say cannot: Unspoken thoughts passing between Sophie and me. Unspoken thoughts passing from Philippe's ghost to Sophie (and then outloud to me). After thinking about it I picked the latter because of the sense I had of Philippe's presence in the room. It was much stronger than eyes on my back.

How could this be? Ghosts don't exist. Things we can't see aren't real.

Ah, but they are. And why shouldn't they be? Think how sight works. It's one of five senses that bring us information from the physical world. Without sight or hearing we'd be like Helen Keller. We'd have a hard time imagining what the world around us is like. But even with 20/20 vision our knowledge is only an approximation of what exists. For example, at this moment what you see is reflected light that has passed through the lenses of your eyes and struck the retinae, which have translated the light into impulses which are sent by the optic nerve to your brain, which translates these impulses into a picture of the page of a book that looks like the thousands of other pages of books you've seen in your life.

But there's so much you don't see. You don't see the comparatively huge distances between paper molecules and ink molecules. You probably don't see the tiny cotton fibers and you don't see microbes squirming around that were left by the last person who picked up this book.

Okay, you say, but scientists can see microbes with a microscope and cotton fibers and even some of the empty space between molecules, so we know all this exists.

Then look around the room for a moment and think about the other things you can't see. For one thing, the space you occupy is filled with television and radio waves.

True, you say, but all it takes is a television and a radio to know they're there.

Yes. And with the right kind of lens or photographic paper you'd also be able to detect infrared light, which the eyes cannot. And x-rays. And gamma rays. And who knows what else.

A lot of things you can't see exist whether you like it or not. Suppose for a moment the instruments to detect them had not been invented yet?

Let's think about a few other invisible things that are unquestionably real. What about a magnetic field? We can't see that or take a picture of it.

We could sprinkle some iron filings on a piece of paper, place a magnet in the middle and shake it gently. Presto, a butterfly shape would form.

How about a gravitational field? That's too big for paper and iron filings, but we know it exists because without it we'd fall off the earth.

What are these fields made of? They aren't material.

And how do they work?

These kinds of fields are curved space. The filings are drawn into the pattern of the space around the magnet. The moon follows the curved space created by the gravitational field around the earth. The earth follows the curved space around the sun and so on.

Space is nothing, right? So how from a Materialist point of view can space be curved?

It can and is because matter isn't really matter (in the sense that we normally think) and empty space isn't empty. Everything is connected and part of one complete whole just as your Stage Four intuition would have you believe. The fact is that twentieth century physics tells us that matter is energy and that energy is matter ($E=mc2$) so contrary to the the way (nineteenth century) Materialists think there really isn't any such thing as solid and separate stuff. Subatomic particles aren't particles in the sense that we are accustomed to thinking, they are packets of energy (quanta) that behave both like waves and like particles. As quantum physicist David Bohm wrote, "Ultimately, the entire universe (with all its particles, including those constituting human beings, their laboratories, observing instruments, etc.) has to be understood as a single undivided whole, in which analysis into separately and independently existent parts has no fundamental status."[3]

24

Anyone wishing to expunge nineteenth century Materialist dogma from their thought processes ought to read Gary Zukav's book, *The Dancing Wu Li Masters.* He explains quantum mechanics without using complicated mathematics. Afterwards they will no longer doubt the sense of connectedness that has started them on Stage Four of their journey. What seems incredible is that so many who work and teach in the life sciences know so little (apparently) of what this branch of science reveals.

For example, Zukav writes:
The astounding discovery awaiting newcomers to physics is that the evidence indicates that subatomic"particles" constantly appear to be making decisions! More than that, the decisions they seem to make are based on decisions made elsewhere. Subatomic particles seem to know *instantaneously* what decisions are made elsewhere, and elsewhere can be as far away as another galaxy! The key word is *instantaneously.* How can a subatomic particle over here know what decision another particle over there has made *at the same time the particle over there makes it?* All the evidence belies the fact that quantum particles are actually particles.[4]

You may be aware that light behaves both as though it consists of waves and of particles (photons). In 1803, Thomas Young demonstrated that light is waves by means of a simple experiment wherein he placed a screen with two vertical slits between a source of light (sunlight coming through a hole in a screen) and a wall. Each slit could be covered with a piece of material. These slits were razor thin, not as wide as the wavelength of the light, and when waves of any kind pass through an opening that is not as wide as they are the waves diffract. This was the case with one slit open. A fuzzy circle of light appeared on the wall. But when both slits were uncovered what was seen were alternating bands of light and darkness, the center band being the brightest. This pattern of light and dark resulted from what is known in wave mechanics as interference. Waves overlap and reinforce each other in some places and in others they cancel each other out. (The bands of light on the wall are where one wave crest overlaps another crest. The dark areas are where a crest and a trough meet and cancel each other.)

In 1905 Albert Einstein published a paper that proved light also behaves like particles and he did so by using the photoelectric effect. When light hits the surface of a metal, it jars electrons loose from the atoms in the metal and sends them flying off as though they had been struck by tiny billiard balls. That light is both waves and particles is a paradox worth considering (according to Newtonian physics this simply cannot be), but what I'm leading up to is an example of subatomic particles (photons in this case) appearing to make decisions. This can be demonstrated using a variation of Young's double slit experiment.

Let's begin. We set up the double slit experiment as before with only one slit open. Suppose this time we fire one photon of light from a gun through the open slit and mark where it hits the wall (using a photographic plate). We notice that it hit a spot that would be dark if both slits were open. Of course, we're only shooting one photon at a time, so there should be no interference. As a matter of curiosity, though, we open the second slit. Without moving the gun we fire another proton at the same spot (through the same slit at the same angle). What happens defies (Materialistic) logic. The photon does not hit where it did before.[5] Somehow it seems to have known the other slit was open and it wasn't supposed to hit in that area.

The question is, how?
Zukav writes:

> . . . the philosophical implication of quantum mechanics is that all of the things in our universe (including us) that appear to exist independently are actually parts of one all-encompassing organic pattern, and that no parts of that pattern are ever really separate from it or from each other.[6]

Pattern with one slit open.

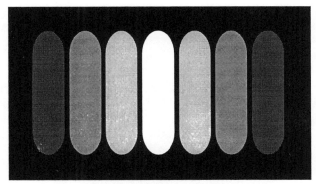

Pattern with two slits open.

So it appears that the entire universe is one huge interconnected field which changes when the second slit is open so that our photon goes where it is supposed to. Once we understand and accept this we are forced to reconsider all sorts of dogmatically held beliefs of Materialism, from the possibility of telepathy and other psychic phenomena to the very nature of life itself. One biochemist has indeed done just this and has developed the field theory into what seems to me a much more logical and intuitively satisfying explanation than can be offered by those holding onto the mechanical view. The biochemist's name is Rupert Sheldrake and his book, *The Rebirth of Nature, The Greening of Science and God,* is a fascinating treatise. He is fully in accord with the notion that the universe is one interconnected field. In the last chapter of his book he notes, anecdotally, that many children have a mystical sense of connection with the natural world which most of us lose as we mature. He quotes a woman, an art teacher, who recounted an experience she had while walking on the Pangbourne Moors at the age of five. She puts into words what I believe many of us have felt at one time or another (but perhaps later dismissed when our "rational" minds again got the upper hand):

> Suddenly I seemed to see the mist as a shimmering gossamer tissue and the harebells, appearing here and there, seemed to shine with a brilliant fire. Somehow I understood that this was the living tissue of life itself, in which all that we call consciousness is embedded, appearing here and there as a shining focus of energy in the more diffused whole. In that moment I knew that I had my special place, as had all other things, animate and so-called inanimate, and that we were all part of this universal tissue which was both fragile yet immensely strong, and utterly good and benificent.[7]

Sounds like an "all-encompassing organic pattern" to me, which is no doubt why Rupert Sheldrake chose this quotation. You may wish to read his theories in the original and I encourage you to do so, but it will be worthwhile to summarize here some of what he has to say.

While physiologists do their best to explain the functioning of plants and animals in mechanistic terms, explanations of some phenomena are sketchy at best. Sheldrake believes the following can be explained by the existence of what he calls morphic fields: Morphogenesis, instinctive behavior, learning, and memory.[8] To this I would add the uncanny correspondences between temperaments, personalities and life choices often made by identical twins even when separated at birth, and an aspect of the evolution of plants and animals which has been recognized over the last twenty or so years: That changes seem to occur rapidly from the standpoint of geological time. A species may remain virtually unchanged for many millennia and then alter dramatically during an epoch when environmental conditions shift. This happens so quickly that scientists are unable to find evidence of the transition. As the eminent authority on evolution, Stephen Jay Gould, wrote, "The extreme rarity of transitional forms in the fossil record persists as the trade secret of paleontology. The evolutionary trees that adorn our textbooks have data only at the tips and nodes of their branches; the rest is inference, however reasonable, not the evidence of fossils."[9]

Sheldrake has broken ranks with his fellow biologists by setting forth the hypothesis that the growth, development and the programmed behavior of organisms are governed by fields which exist much like fields of gravity or electromagnetism, and that these fields change and evolve as a species changes and evolves. He calls them "morphic fields," the word "morphic" indicating shape or form. Indeed, these fields contain the collective memory of the entire species. He writes:

> The fields of a given species, such as the giraffe, have evolved; they are inherited by present giraffes from previous giraffes. They contain a kind of collective memory on which each member of the species draws and to which it in turn contributes. The formative activity of the fields is not determined

by timeless mathematical laws--although the fields can to some extent be modeled mathematically--but by the actual forms taken up by previous members of the species. The more often a pattern of development is repeated, the more probable it is that it will be followed again. The fields are the means by which the habits of the species are built up, maintained, and inherited.[10]

Sheldrake calls his hypothesis formative causation and it was first proposed in 1981 in his book *A New Science of Life* and developed further in *The Presence of the Past* (1988). It suggests that self-organizing systems exist at all levels of complexity, including molecules, crystals, cells, tissues, organisms, and societies of organisms (such as ants and bees).[11]

Consideration of the existence of morphic fields provides a compelling explanation of how morphogenesis works. The genes supply the right building blocks of protein and the field provides the blueprint. Without this governing (morphogenetic) field scientists are hard pressed to explain something as simple as the shapes of your arms and legs and feet. (They believe the information is encoded in the genes but they aren't certain where or how.) Think about it. Your limbs are made of muscle cells and nerve cells and bone cells and so on. They use the same building materials but have different shapes, just as differently shaped buildings can be constructed with the same type of bricks but with different blueprints.

These fields may also explain a phenomena of memory which currently has neuroscientists puzzled: where it is located in the brain. One way research on this subject has been conducted is to train an animal to do something and then to cut out parts of its brain in an effort to find where the the memory was stored. As Sheldrake writes, "But even after large chunks of their brains have been removed--in some experiments over 60 percent--the hapless animals can often remember what they were trained to do before the operation."[12] Several theories have been put forth to explain this including backup systems and holograms, but the obvious one in light of Sheldrake's hypothesis is that the memory may not be in the brain at all. Scientists have been looking in the wrong place. To quote Sheldrake again, "A search inside your TV set for traces of the programs you watched last week would be doomed to failure for the same reason: The set tunes in to TV transmissions but does not store them."[13] In other words, the brain is our physical link to the memory located in our individual morphic field.

The implications for the explanation of instinctive behavior are obvious as they are also for the behavior of societal insects, fishes and birds. For example we've all seen swarms of gnats, schools of fish, or flocks of birds behaving as though they were a single organism as they glide through the air or water, turning and diving as though they form one unified whole. Spend some time at an aquarium watching a school of fish. Something is sure to cause a minor explosion in their midst producing momentary chaos as individuals scatter a short distance from their original positions. But within seconds they will regroup and become a single moving organism once more.

The behavior of some species is truly amazing, or would be without Sheldrake's theory. Key West silver-sided fish, for example, will organize themselves around a barracuda in a shape that seems dictated by risk. The distance between the school and the barracuda is widest at the predator's mouth and narrowest at the tail, where the threat of being eaten is the least.

In the world of insects, African termites, which are blind, rebuild tunnels and arches from both sides of a breach and meet up perfectly in the middle, and they can do this even when the two sides have been separated by a large steel plate that is several feet wider and higher than the termitary and placed so that it divides the mound.[14]

Concerning identical twins, the possibility they may share a morphogenetic field in some way might account for physical similarities and behavioral choices that scientists have been unable to explain. Beyond the fact of looking alike, which sharing the same field would explain, almost every identical twin can relate anecdotal evidence of a special, perhaps even "psychic" connection with his or her sibling.

A strict Materialist will argue that this sort of thing can easily be accounted for by the fact of having been raised together. But what about identical twins who were not raised together? In 1979 a study was conducted by the University of Minnesota in which twins separated for years were investigated and subjected to medical and psychological tests. The results demonstrated astonishing affinities between the subjects even though some had never met. The example of Jim Spring and Jim Lewis, twins who never knew each other and were raised in different Ohio towns, is one case in point. Both married and divorced women called Linda and chose a woman named Betty as a second wife. Each of the two twins named their sons James Allan and each had a favorite dog named Toy. Both had identical blood pressure, sleep and heart-beat patterns. At the age of 18 both had suffered intermittent migraine headaches. Their drinking and smoking habits were identical. Both men chewed their finger nails.[15]

Be all this as it may, what must be mind-boggling about Sheldrake's hypothesis to those accustomed to thinking of heredity as working solely by the passing of genes through egg and sperm is this: *Acquired* characteristics can be passed from one generation to the next. This might explain the rapidity of changes in organisms when environmental shifts occur. Natural selection would be given a boost enabling a species to adapt more readily, not only because hard-learned survival behavior could be passed on, but because the information would not be passed solely from parent to offspring. As new behavioral habits or physical characteristics change the morphic field of the entire species, all its members would become affected.

The implications of Sheldrake's hypothesis are incredibly widespread. We will examine only those which relate to our quest of spiritual growth, but to give an inkling of those falling outside the parameters of this book, consider this: During this century athletes have achieved ever higher levels of excellence in everything from Olympic track and field to tennis. Improvements in diet, equipment, training techniques and coaching have certainly played a big role. One now must also consider whether memories located in morphic fields may also be a factor. According to the theory, what has been learned by the pioneers in a sport would become embedded in the morphic field of humanity and this should make learning (as well as body and muscle coordination) easier for future participants.

Sheldrake's hypothesis of formative causation is controversial but it is testable by experiment. For example, when a newly synthesized organic chemical is crystallized for the first time (a new drug for instance) there would be no morphic resonance from prior crystals since none of the type existed before. Of the many ways the substance might crystallize one actually does, and a new morphic field comes into existence. The next time the substance is crystallized morphic resonance from the first crystals will make the same pattern more probable. A cumulative memory will be built up as the process is repeated. The pattern will become more habitual and the substance will form more readily each time (no matter in what laboratory or location in the world the crystallization takes place). This tendency is indeed a known fact in the scientific community but other explanations usually are offered to explain it. The most common is that fragments of previous crystals are transferred from laboratory to laboratory on the hair or clothes of chemists.[16] Controlled experiments would be simple enough to conduct that eliminate this possibility. It is my hope that someone will take up this challenge.

Because we in the Fourth Stage sense the connectedness of all things and have trouble buying into the Materialist point of view, what Sheldrake says makes sense to us on an intuitive level. Behind and supporting the physical matter of the universe is an enormous field. Mankind has its own field within this larger field as does each species of plant or animal. Everything (the earth, crystals, toads) and everyone has their own personal field within the larger field of the group. All fields, from that of the entire universe down to that of a single molecule, are interconnected because in reality there is only one field.

This concept fits our personal experience. That we

are connected and one underneath the appearance of physical reality could explain the feeling of eyes on our back, waking up the instant before the alarm goes off, the possibility of tarot cards predicting a chance meaning with a blond young man, and the existence of Philippe's ghost (his morphic field). Before I read about Sheldrake's hypothesis I had already sensed something like this. In one of my novels, *Out of Body, Into Mind*, the heroine comes to the same realization. She has had an out of body experience and glimpses the Eternal. The following takes place after she has returned and described the experience to her boyfriend. (He has just told her she must have been dreaming.)

> I decided it didn't matter what Jeff or anyone else thought and turned my attention instead to the display of nature all around. A remnant of the glow of the light from the other side must still have been with me because I felt in awe as I took in the scene. We were passing giant bamboo, mountain palms, chestnut and mahogany trees, and were almost engulfed by foliage. It was hot and bugs swarmed and normally I'd have felt uncomfortable because of the temperature and the insects and the humidity or perhaps even frightened by what I would have seen as an alien environment. Instead, I had the sensation of being part of it, of being one with it, the same feeling I'd had when I viewed the sunset from the motorcycle. The life force was expressing herself and I was seeing the outside of what was inside, the physical manifestation of the invisible: one thing, completely and utterly connected. Then it came to me with the same unequivocal sense of knowing Jean-Luc had experienced during his revelation. I'd learned the secret of life. Of course, I thought, why hadn't I grasped it before? It is *the urge to become* I'd sensed in myself for as long as I could remember, which I now realized was the light's desire to express and experience itself. A vision flashed in my mind of a cave, a cavern like we have in the Blue Ridge Mountains of Virginia with

millions of stalactites and stalagmites forming
intricate and wondrous patterns glistening with tiny
droplets of water. The whole was nature and each
stalactite or stalagmite a separate soul, or species of
plant or animal. Each had its own identity but was
also part of the larger formation of rock. Every drop
of water was a current life leaving in its path a tiny
deposit which helped shape the species, or in the
case of humans--the soul. At that moment I
understood that the realm of my father's Higher Self
was a metaphor his mind had created just as mine
had created this cavern, and that his life, my life and
your life are like those water droplets. They are
expressions of the light and cause something larger
to grow, a universe that is becoming. They are sent
forth as knights were sent forth to the Crusades.

The heroine's vision of course is my vision. It is a
vision of one giant connected whole that is constantly being
expanded by the unique experiences and insights realized by
each new life that ventures forth on the physical plane. It
was brought about by the urge to become, by the desire of
Infinite Intelligence to know and to replicate Itself and it
continues to evolve because of this. We will explore this
vision in the chapters that lie ahead and determine the
implications of its characteristics for you as you move
forward on your journey.

Then you will know the truth,
and the truth will set you free.

John 8:32

Chapter Two: The Universe, What and Why?

"Anyone who has had an experience of mystery knows that there is a dimension of the universe that is not that which is available to his senses," Joseph Campbell said in *The Power of Myth.*[1]   Indeed, the existence of what we wish to examine has been recognized by mystics of all religions down through the ages, and though at times they have caught glimpses of it, have perhaps basked in its radiance and experienced an incredible sensation of all-knowing, the nature of the unseen has remained a mystery to one and all.

We are embarking on a quest, you and I, which has never before been successfully completed: to come to know and to the extent humanly possible understand the unseen reality behind and supportive of the physical plane.

Are we foolhardy to try? Perhaps. But if Rupert Sheldrake is on the mark, there are some things we do know about the invisible. First, it seems certain that the underlying message of all mythologies is correct: an invisible plane supports and informs the visible. According to Sheldrake's hypothesis, it is the universal field and morphic fields within the universal field which give form to the physical world, from the shape of the earth and its gravitational field to the shape of your nose and the structure of a crystal. The field does not remain static but is constantly changing and evolving. The entire morphic history of a species is contained by its field and can be seen unfolding in the growth of an embryo. The collective memory of a species and instinctive behavior are components. Individual memories are contained in the fields of individual organisms. Brains are devices which retrieve these memories. A field can transcend the individuals of a species. For instance, fields unite colonies of organisms such as certain ants, bees, birds and fish. Thus the entire colony operates as one. Indeed, it may be possible that identical twins share a field at some level just as at a higher level we as individuals share the field of our species and at an even higher level still, the planet. Taken to the highest of all levels the entire field of the universe can be viewed as one living organism of which all others are part: the earth, each individual species, mankind, and every individual plant or animal including you and me. This mirrors the experience of the artist described in chapter one when she was walking on the Pangbourne Moors at the age of five. It mirrors the sensation of oneness experienced by mystics throughout the ages. Of this, William Johnston, author of *Silent Music* wrote:

> But there is a human question which psychology never asks and which leads people to religion; namely, what is at the deepest realm of the psyche? What is the basis or centre or root of all? Put in Jungian terms I might ask: When I go beyond the ego, beyond the personal unconscious, beyond the collective unconscious, beyond the archetypes, what do I find? And in answer to this all the great religions speak of a mystery which they call by various names: the Buddha nature, Brahman and Atman, the divine spark, the ground of being, the centre of the

soul, the kingdom of God, the image of God and so on. They use different terms; but all I believe, are pointing towards a single reality.[2]

You and I now know it is the larger organism of the universe of which we are part. We are each an aspect of this whole just as a foot or a nose is an aspect of our body. When we recognize this, truly feel it in our being, we are compelled to change the way we view all that surrounds us. As Joseph Campbell said, "But then, when the center of the heart is touched, and a sense of compassion awakened with another person or creature, and you realize that you and that other are in some sense creatures of the one life in being, a whole new stage of life in the spirit opens out."[3]

Indeed it seems to me that a goal of our spiritual journey ought to be to achieve this realization on a gut level. As we will see, this appears to be what the Buddhists seek in their quest for Nirvana, what the Hindus seek in the ultimate union with Brahman, and perhaps what Christ had in mind when he spoke of entering the Kingdom of God.

How can we accomplish this?

As a starting place let's explore some basic metaphysical questions. Why does this organism of the universe with which we are one exist? Where is it headed? What is its purpose? What role does mankind play? What role do you and I play as individuals?

Not long ago I came across what I consider to be an amusing view concerning the goal of life on earth. In a book not yet published at this writing, biologist Richard Dawkins considers the matter of cheetahs and gazelles. What is the purpose of a cheetah? Of a gazelle? We might conclude that the fleet-footed cheetah is superbly designed to hunt gazelles and that gazelles on the other hand are clearly optimized to evade cheetahs. This being the case, what, Dawkins asks, is the overall goal of such an apparently self-defeating scheme? Certainly it goes beyond both the cheetah and the gazelle, and for that matter the brief lives of all living creatures.

Dawkins concludes that the central purpose of evolution is the survival of DNA, not of the creatures that are the DNA's temporary expression.[4]   According to this theory DNA has been blindly pursuing a plan of survival and reproduction of itself ever since the first molecule of RNA, DNA's elder cousin, got itself replicated in the stew of chemicals on the primitive earth which we discussed earlier.

One might expect a Materialist to come to a conclusion such as this since for them nothing exists they cannot see. Knowing as we do about the field, however, Dawkins is for us rather like some Marshall McKuhan of biology concluding that the medium (DNA) is the message (of the field).

It is quite possible that no purpose exists outside of the desire of the universe to express and experience itself. The cheetah and the gazelle simply may be part of the dance. To me this would be a more logical and satisfying explanation than mindless double helixes replicating themselves ad nauseam. Indeed, this idea of self-expression seems to be the prevailing view in eastern religions and in pantheism. The universe just is. It doesn't have a purpose beyond its own amusement.

Alan Watts, a twentieth century philosopher and interpreter of Zen Buddhism, answered children when they asked questions such as why they are here, where the universe came from, where people go when they die and so on with a parable about God playing hide and seek. Watts would tell them God enjoys the game but has no one outside himself to play with since he is all that is. He overcomes this problem of being all, and therefore not having any playmates, by pretending he is not himself. Instead he pretends that he is me and you and all the other people and the animals and rocks and stars and planets and plants and in doing so has wonderful and wondrous adventures. These adventures are more like dreams because when he awakes they will disappear. He writes:

> Now when God plays hide and
> pretends that he is you and I, he does it
> so well that it takes him a long time to
> remember where and how he hid himself.
> But that's the whole fun of it--just what

40

he wanted to do. He doesn't want to find himself too quickly, for that would spoil the game. That is why it is so difficult for you and me to find out that we are God in disguise, pretending not to be himself. But when the game has gone on long enough, all of us will wake up, stop pretending, and remember that we are all one single Self--the God who is all that there is and who lives for ever and ever.[5]

It will no doubt be shocking to some to think of themselves as God, but Watts was talking about the core essence that is beyond the ego and deeper within than the personal unconscious, the collective unconscious, the archetypes and so on as was William Johnson in the prior quotation. As Joseph Campbell said, "You see, there are two ways of thinking 'I am God.' If you think, 'I here, in my physical presence and in my temporal character, am God,' then you are mad and have short-circuited the experience. You are God, not in your ego, but in your deepest being, where you are at one with the nondual transcendent."[6]

By the way, up until now I have avoided using the term God when speaking of the field because it is a confusing word, often loaded with emotional baggage, that means different things to different people. In our western culture it generally conveys the Stage Two idea of the big cop in the sky. For Stage Four Christians, God is present (immanent) in all things. He is like the field itself. Without Him nothing else could exist. Yet He would continue to exist even if nothing else did. Alan Watts clearly was using the word in the transcendental (universal field) sense, as was Joseph Campbell. From here on I'll use the word in the same way unless otherwise indicated, and later I'll introduce a new term of my own, the Big Dreamer.

If each of us is God we will eventually wake up, according to Alan Watts, and find out what our purpose is (if there is one other than playing hide and seek). Nevertheless, in an effort to get our minds around what we're about in the meantime, let us continue to explore the possibilities.

We have learned that the field constantly is changing and evolving. This seems to argue against the concepts of determinism and predestination which have come in and out of vogue among theologians over the years. Nevertheless, a question we might ask is whether the field is moving toward a predetermined goal or state of being. Is the field on a path to a particular destination? Does it know the way and simply is unfolding? Is there a road map so that every thing and every event is known in advance?

Apparently not. There may be a final end toward which the field is headed, but it does not appear that the way to this has been known from the beginning because the most direct path is not being followed. For example, thousands of species of animals and plants have become extinct with the result that thousands of dead ends have been reached. What purpose, for example, did the dinosaurs serve?

Okay. They contributed to the oil and coal reserves. Without them we may have burned up all the forests by now.

Well, then, how about the Irish elk? His thirteen-foot-wide antlers certainly must have looked grand standing atop his majestic head, but the only purpose they served was the extinction of the animal who wore them when his environment shifted.

Charles Darwin observed that evolution does not move ahead in a way that seems to have been predetermined. He expounded this in his writings on orchids. He maintained that self-fertilization is a poor strategy for long-term survival since offspring carry only the genes (and I would add, perhaps only the morphic field) of a single parent. As a result, plants with flowers that have both male and female parts usually evolve mechanisms to ensure cross-pollination. Darwin used orchids to illustrate the astonishing variety of ways which they have evolved to attract insects, to insure pollen adheres to a visitor and that once attached the pollen will come in contact with the female parts of the next orchid visited.

Orchids use the common components of ordinary flowers to fabricate the intricate devices that are required, components which are usually fitted for very different functions. So, orchids are jury-rigged, so to speak, from a limited set of available parts, proof they are evolved from ordinary flowers.[7] Thus, neither the course of their evolution nor even their existence as a species seems to have been planned from the beginning of time.

Another example is the panda's thumb.

If you've ever been to the National Zoo in Washington, you've probably watched the giant pandas sitting around eating bamboo leaves. They take stalk after stalk and slide them between thumb and forefinger stripping them, then pop this mouth-watering high-fiber food in their mouths. You may have wondered how these big guys got thumbs since Primates are the ones with opposing digits and pandas belong to the family Procyonidae (raccoons, kinkajous, etc.) of the order Carnivora, one of the hallmarks of which is that all five digits on the front paw point forward with claws for ripping flesh.

On close inspection you'll find that the panda's thumb is not a thumb at all but a "complex structure formed by marked enlargement of a (wrist) bone and an extensive rearrangement of musculature."[8] Not having the thumb needed to make bamboo eating easy, the panda took what he had to work with and evolved one of a makeshift variety. As Stephen Jay Gould writes, "The panda's thumb provides an elegant zoological counterpart to Darwin's orchids. An engineer's best solution is debarred by history. The panda's true thumb is committed to another role, too specialized for a different function to become an opposable, manipulating digit. So the panda must use parts on hand and settle for an enlarged wrist bone and a somewhat clumsy, but quite workable, solution."[9] Gould also writes, "Odd arrangements and funny solutions are the proof of evolution--paths that a sensible God would never tread but that a natural process, constrained by history, follows perforce."[10]

From this we might conclude that either the field does not know where it is headed, or perhaps, that the specific route it follows to get there doesn't really matter. All it is interested in for the moment are solutions that work and thereby keep the game alive.

So where can we turn for clues as to what the field is up to?

Why not to those who have pondered this question deeply throughout the ages? In the final chapter of his book, *The Religions of Man,* Huston Smith came to a conclusion which may prove instructive. He writes, "Does not each (religion) contain some version of the Golden Rule? Do they not all regard man's self-centeredness to be the source of his troubles and seek to help him in its conquest? Does not each acknowledge a universal Divine Ground from which man has sprung and in relation to which his true good is to be sought? If all truth essential to salvation can be found in one religion, it can also be found in each of the other great ones."[11]

Joseph Campbell echoed these when he said, "All religions have been true for their time. If you can recognize the enduring aspect of their truth and separate it from the temporal applications, you've got it."[12]

What do the various religions say about where things are headed and why? Is there one or are there components of one or more that fit what we know about the field?

Let's take a look first at Hinduism, one of the oldest and largest religions (about 500 million followers). It is thought to date from about 4000 years ago and unlike Christianity, Islam and Buddhism, had no single founder. Hinduism came into being over time in the Indus River valley and other parts of western India and is completely decentralized with no hierarchy of clergy and no supreme authority. As Hinduism developed it continually absorbed and reinterpreted the beliefs and practices of the different people with whom it came in contact with the result that many differences exist from one geographical area to another. Making generalizations is perhaps unwise as a result and is certainly fraught with possible pitfalls, but at the risk of incurring the wrath of some of its practitioners I will plunge ahead and do so anyway.

Hindus believe that behind the ever-changing physical world is one universal, unchanging, everlasting spirit known as Brahman. The soul, or Atman, of every being in the universe, including the gods, is part of this spirit and inseparable from it. (It has been likened to a cup of water in the ocean, part of it yet separate at the same time.)

This sounds like the field, doesn't it?

Literally hundreds of gods exist but they are all of the same divinity, just as humans are, because everyone and everything is part of the oneness of Brahman. Only the veil of maya (the illusory world of the senses) prevents man from understanding and grasping this.

Let me point out that the idea of a multiplicity of gods is very different from our western idea of the big cop in the sky, God with a big G, since Hindu gods are not prime movers but arise out of the field (Brahman) as channels for its energy. As a metaphor this does not seem so very far from what we know about the field.

So where do Hindus think things are headed? And what is the purpose of it all?

According to Hindu belief the course of the universe through time is cyclical. Every event has happened before and will happen again. This applies not only to the life of the individual in his rebirths but also to the history of society, the lives of the gods, and the evolution of the entire cosmos. Each person has lived many times and the fortunes of the soul in each rebirth are determined by its behavior in former lives. This is the law of karma (cause and effect) and it states that no sin ever goes unpunished and no virtue remains unrewarded. If a man does not receive his punishment or his reward in this life, he will do so in a succeeding one.

On the surface it seems unfair that we would be punished or rewarded for something we did in another persona in another lifetime we don't remember. But perhaps if we envision the entire field of mankind as the soul and each individual (past, present and future) as an incarnation, the concept makes sense. In the end, all our actions will equal out. Even so, the Hindu interpretation may simply be an ingenious way to keep order, or in the words of Joseph Campbell, a "temporal application."

Hindu society is fragmented into several thousand

45

castes ranging in size from a few dozen to a few thousand people. A Hindu is born into one caste and may not change it during his lifetime. He must marry within his caste and may possibly carry on his caste's traditional occupation. All the castes in a region are ranked according to social status, with Brahmins or priests at the top of the hierarchy. As a consequence of the doctrine of karma the majority of Hindus feel that one's position in the hierarchy is a direct result of one's behavior in previous lives. If a man performs the duties of his caste diligently he may improve his caste position in a future birth. For most Hindus this is the goal of life. But to us westerners, particularly in America where class mobility is the norm, towing the line with the goal of improving our social and economic position next time around hardly seems worth the effort. As is the case with the highest caste of Hindu, we need something more to strive for. This leads to the question, what do the people in this category seek?

The top stratum is concerned with Moksha, or release from rebirth. There are three ways to break out of the cycle of reincarnation: 1.) A life of deeds appropriate to one's station in life. All actions must be performed selflessly, without regard to gratification of personal desire. This leads to detachment from the self and union with Brahman. 2.) Uncompromising devotion and faith to a personal god. This brings the believer closer to Brahman and can generate the insight of the unity of all things necessary to see beyond maya. When this happens the soul is released. 3.) Direct insight into the ultimate truth of the universe (the unity of all things). This requires renunciation of all worldly attachments and a rigorous course of ascetic and mystical practice such as yoga.

So it appears that the ultimate goal and destination for Hindus, where they believe all are headed and will someday arrive if they persevere, is what Alan Watts told us earlier. They will wake up and realize they each are God (or in the terminology of Hinduism, Brahman). The illusion that they are not, the sense that they are separate and distinct individuals who exist apart is the illusion (maya) which must be overcome.

Buddhism, which came out of Hinduism, teaches followers that they don't have to work their way up caste by caste from one reincarnation to the next for this to happen. Buddhists believe an individual does not even have to die.

Buddha (which means, "The Enlightened One") was a historical figure who lived about 500 bc. His given name was Siddhartha Gautama and the story goes that at his birth it was predicted he would become either a great emperor or a great teacher. Four signs would show him which course he should follow.

Siddhartha's father preferred the emperor role for him and took great pains to prevent him from seeing signs that would influence him to be a teacher. As a result the boy was raised in luxury. But at the age of 29 he finally saw the signs his father hoped would never come his way: old age (a decrepit old man), sickness (a diseased man), death (a corpse), and true serenity (a wandering religious mendicant). Siddhartha realized the first three signs stood for the presence of suffering in the world which he perceived as doubly terrible because he believed as did other Hindus that man was continually reborn. Suffering was for all eternity. As a result he left his family and set out searching for enlightenment. He took up with five ascetics, but after six years got fed up and decided to sit under a tree until enlightenment came. He sat there for 49 days during which time he withstood the temptations of Mara, the Buddhist devil. On the morning of the forty-nineth day he achieved enlightenment and union with Nirvana, which is the ultimate detachment from the world. With Nirvana comes end to suffering, the ultimate goal of all Buddhists.

Okay. But what do the Buddha's teachings tell us about the unseen?

Almost nothing. The fact is Buddha refused to discuss metaphysics and never told his followers whether he believed there was life after death for those who had achieved Nirvana or whether the world was eternal, or where it might all be headed. Apparently, he did not want his followers distracted from the hard road toward enlightenment. This is illustrated in Buddha's parable of the arrow:

Beyond Skepticism

It is as if a man had been wounded
by an arrow thickly smeared with poison,
and his friends and kinsmen were to get a
surgeon to heal him, and he were to say, I
will not have this arrow pulled out until I
know by what man I was wounded, whether
he is of the warrior caste, or a brahmin, or
of the agricultural, or the lowest caste. Or if
he were to say, I will not have this arrow
pulled out until I know of what name of
family the man is;--or whether he is tall,
or short, or of middle height; or whether
he is black, or dark, or yellowish; or whether
he comes from such and such a village, or
town, or city; or until I know whether the
bow with which I was wounded was a
chapa or a kodanda, or until I know whether
the bow-string was of swallow-wort, or
bamboo fiber, or sinew, or hemp or of
milk-sap tree, or until I know whether the
shaft was from a wild or cultivated plant; or
whether it was feathered from a vulture's
wing or a heron's or a hawk's, or a peacock's;
or whether it was wrapped round with the
sinew of an ox, or of a buffalo, or of a
ruru-deer, or of a monkey; or a razor-arrow,
or an iron arrow, or a calf-tooth arrow.
Before knowing all this, that man would die.

Similarly, it is not on the view that
the world is eternal, that it is finite, that the
body and soul are distinct or that the Buddha
exists after death that a religious life depends.
Whether these views or their opposites are held,
there is still rebirth, there is old age, there is
death, and grief, lamentation, suffering, sorrow,
and despair. . . .

I have not spoken to these views
because they do not conduce to absence of
passion, tranquility, and Nirvana.

And what have I explained? Suffering

have I explained, the cause of suffering, the destruction of suffering, and the path that leads to the destruction of suffering have I explained. For this is useful.

Therefore, my disciples, consider as unexplained what I have not explained, and consider as explained what I have explained.[13]

Nirvana is a kind of peace, a state of mind or consciousness, rather than a place. One does not have to die to reach it. It seems likely it comes from knowing on a gut level what you and I know on an intellectual level: that we and the field are one. Once we know and experience this deep down, the pain of existence vanishes and we begin acting out of this knowledge. In the words of Joseph Campbell, "(Nirvana) is right here, in the midst of the turmoil of life. It is the state you find when you are no longer driven to live by compelling desires, fears, and social commitments, when you have found your center of freedom and can act by choice out of that. Voluntary action out of this center is the action of the bodhisattvas--joyful participation in the sorrows of the world. You are not grabbed, because you have released yourself from the grabbers of fear, lust, and duties. These are the rulers of the world."[14]

A bodhisattva, by the way, is an individual who has achieved Nirvana, or at least come to the brink of it, but has turned away to participate voluntarily in the sorrows of life. He has come back into the game so to speak in order to help others find their way out of it.[15]

So how does one reach Nirvana? According to the Buddha one must know and live by his "Four Noble Truths":

1) *The Noble Truth of Suffering:* suffering is inherent in all life in the experiences of birth, old age, sickness and death; in union with the unpleasant; in separation from the pleasant; in failing to obtain what one wishes; in clinging to existence.

2) *The Noble Truth of the Cause of Suffering:* craving or desire. The craving for lust, for existence, for

non-existence. In a nutshell, the craving or desire for any and every thing. If we crave the trappings of the world we cannot escape from the world. We will be reborn.

3) *The Noble Truth of the Cessation of Suffering,* which is the cessation of craving by the forsaking and relinquishing of craving so that one may be set free.

4) *The Noble Truth of the Path that Leads to the Cessation of Suffering (The Eightfold Path):* right view, right thought, right speech, right action, right livelihood, right effort, right mindfulness, right concentration. By following the path, craving is extinguished and deliverance from suffering (into the state of Nirvana) is achieved.

It seems to me that this emphasis on suffering and a desire to escape from it may to a large degree be a product of the place and time the Buddha lived, another "temporal application." And no wonder. If you want to see the type of suffering the he and his followers wanted to avoid, you do not have to travel back in time to the world of 500 B.C. A trip to the India of today or to practically any Third World country will do the trick. Gruesome is hardly an adequate word to describe it.

For us in the West a more accurate description of our condition can be found in the first three words of Scott Peck's book, *The Road Less Traveled:* "Life is difficult." Once we accept this, things usually don't seem nearly as bad as they did when we thought life was supposed to be a bowl of cherries. Life may be difficult, but difficulty is not nearly as unpleasant as suffering. Difficulty we can live with. Without difficulties how would we know when times are good?

As Kahil Gibran wrote in *The Prophet:*

Your joy is your sorrow unmasked.
And the selfsame well from which
your laughter rises was oftentimes filled
with your tears.
And how else can it be?
The deeper that sorrow carves into
your being, the more joy you can contain.
Is not the cup that holds your wine

50

the very cup that was burned in the potter's oven?
    And is not the lute that soothes your
spirit, the very wood that was hollowed with
knives?
    When you are joyous, look deep
into your heart and you shall find it is only
that which has given you sorrow that is
giving you joy.
    When you are sorrowful look again
in your heart, and you shall see that in truth
you are weeping for that which has been your
delight.
    Some of you say, "Joy is greater
than sorrow," and others say, "Nay, sorrow
is the greater."
    But I say unto you, they are
inseparable.
    Together they come, and when one
sits alone with you at your board, remember
that the other is asleep upon your bed.[16]

Joy and sorrow are both integral to the game. Of course all of us would like to minimize our difficulties. But I have a feeling life would be dull if we did away with them entirely. It would be nice, however, to jettison the sense of frustration we often live with in this modern world. Perhaps that gut-level realization of oneness with the field that leads to Nirvana for the Buddhists can enable us to do just that. Moments of joy would become more intense. They would be savored. Sorrows would be looked upon philosophically. Indeed, a sense of union with the field would empower us. By shedding the ego and getting into harmony with all that is and with our higher selves, we would be in position to live the fulfilling life we were born to live.

Alan Watts said of the realization:

In immediate contrast to the old feeling,
there is indeed a certain passivity to the
sensation, as if you were a leaf blown along

by the wind, until you realize that you are
both the leaf and the wind. The world outside
your skin is just as much you as the world
inside: they move together inseparably, and at
first you feel a little out of control because
the world outside is so much vaster than the
world inside. Yet you soon discover that you
are able to go ahead with ordinary activities--to
work and make decisions as ever, though somehow
this is less of a drag. Your body is no longer
a corpse which the ego has to animate and lug
around. There is a feeling of the ground holding
you up, and of hills lifting you when you climb
them. Air breathes itself in and out of your lungs,
and instead of looking and listening, light and
sound come to you on their own . Eyes see and ears
hear as wind blows and water flows. All space
becomes your mind. Time carries you along like
a river, but never flows out of the present: the
more it goes the more it stays, and you no longer
have to fight or kill it.[17]

Where other than Hinduism and Buddhism can we
look for instruction on how to achieve this? Let's take a look
first at the life and teachings of a carpenter who lived some
2000 years ago in the Middle East.

Whatever you may think of the religion which has
grown up as a result of his life, the man named Jesus
appears to have been one who lived as a true bodhisattva.
He chose to participate voluntarily in the sorrows of life in
order to teach others and lead them out of their suffering.
By the age of 30 at the beginning of his ministry there can be
little doubt he had achieved what Alan Watts just spoke of
and what the Buddha called Nirvana. When we recognize
this, many of the sayings attributed to him come clearly into
focus. (All of the excerpts here by the way are from the NIV
translation of the Bible.)

Jesus clearly believes that all of us are one:

Whoever welcomes this little child in my
name welcomes me; and whoever welcomes me
welcomes the one who sent me. For he who
is least among you all--he is the greatest.

Luke 9:48

That what he called the kingdom of God and what
we have labeled the field is not outside you. You and it are
the same:

The kingdom of God does not come with your
careful observation, nor will people say,
'Here it is,' or 'There it is,' because the
kingdom of God is within you.

Luke 17:20-21

That one of the requisites for achieving it is to set
aside our egotistic nature and to adopt a position of humility:

I tell you the truth, anyone who will not
receive the kingdom of God like a little child
will never enter it.

Mark 10:15

That with it comes the realization that you are one
with the transcendent:

They all asked, "Are you the Son of God?"
He replied, "You are right in saying I am."

Luke 22:70

Joseph Campbell said, "Jesus was a historical person
who realized in himself that he and what he called the Father
were one, and he lived out of that knowledge of the
Christhood of his nature."[18]
Most of what he taught falls into one of three areas.

53

That faith brings peace. That the power of belief is awesome. That love and service toward fellow man are the ways to the kingdom.

By faith he appears to have meant an attitude of surrender and openness to the transcendent:

> Therefore I tell you, do not worry about
> your life, what you will eat or drink; or
> about your body, what you will wear. Is
> not life more important than food, and the
> body more important than clothes? Look at
> the birds of the air; they do not sow or
> reap or store away in barns, and yet your
> heavenly Father feeds them. Are you not
> much more valuable than they?

Matthew 6:25-26

On the power of belief he said:

Everything is possible for him who believes.

Mark 9:23

> I tell you the truth, if anyone says to this
> mountain, 'Go, throw yourself into the sea,'
> and does not doubt in his heart but believes
> that what he says will happen, it will be done
> for him. Therefore I tell you, whatever you
> ask for in prayer, believe that you have received
> it, and it will be yours.

Mark 11:23-24

About love and service:

> "The most important (commandment)," answered
> Jesus, "is this: 'Hear, O Israel, the Lord our
> God, the Lord is one. Love the Lord your God

54

with all your heart and with all your soul and
with all your mind and with all your strength.
The second is this: Love your neighbor as
yourself. There is no commandment greater
than these."

Mark 12:29-31

... whoever wants to be great among you must
be your servant, and whoever wants to be first
must be slave of all.

Mark 10:43-44

Do not judge, and you will not be judged. Do
not condemn, and you will not be condemned.
Forgive, and you will be forgiven. Give,
and it will be given to you. A good measure,
pressed down, shaken together and running
over, will be poured into your lap. For
with the measure you use, it will be measured
to you.

Luke 6:37-38

One of the things which baffles non-Christians is the
Christian doctrine that Jesus was God incarnate. We have
seen, however, that in a sense we all are. The enigma comes
when we think of him as the Big Cop in the flesh.
According to Karen Armstrong, author of *A History of
God,* the doctrine that Jesus actually had been God come to
earth in human form was not finalized until over three
hundred years after his death.[19]   Even Saint Paul, who
supplied many of the writings of the New Testament and did
more than any other individual to get the Christian Church
off the ground, never called Jesus "God."[20]   He called him
"the Son of God," but this is a Jewish figure of speech of
the time. For example, consider the following quotation of
Jesus:

> You have heard that it was said, 'Love your
> neighbor and hate your enemy.' But I tell you:
> Love your enemies and pray for those who
> persecute you, that you may be *sons of your
> Father in heaven.* He causes his sun to rise
> on the evil and the good, and sends rain on
> the righteous and the unrighteous.

Matthew 5:43-45

I've added the italics above for emphasis. Not only does Jesus believe we all can be "sons of God," but this quotation seems to demonstrate his understanding that no one and no thing exists apart from the field. We all participate in the dance and are part of the unified whole whether or not we behave the way we ought toward fellow man. The key to entering the kingdom of God (realizing on a gut level we are at one with the field) is to rise above the fray and to see things and act from the unified point of view. We wouldn't get angry with our foot or elbow if they weren't behaving the way we thought they should.

In reading the Gospels keep in mind that Jesus was a Jew who was preaching to Jews. Much of what is said must be understood in this context. Saint Paul was also Jewish but even though he viewed things from a Jewish perspective he believed Christ's message was meant for the Gentiles as well and that salvation through Christ was open to all.

The essential doctrine preached by Saint Paul was that man is by nature imperfect. This has been the case since Adam first sinned and got booted out of Eden. The Jews were God's chosen people and they had been given laws to live by that would lead to their salvation if they obeyed them to the letter. The Catch 22 was that no matter how hard a person tried to obey the Jewish laws (and there were a ton of them) no one could make it into the kingdom of God on his record because he simply could not go through life with a perfect score. So, God sent Jesus into the world to atone for man's sins. Jesus was perfect. He was like a lamb without sin who was sacrificed on an altar. Paul believed he suffered for the rest of us who are imperfect.

Here is a portion of what he wrote on this subject:

> But now a righteousness from God apart
> from law, has been made known, to which
> the Law and the Prophets testify. This
> righteousness from God comes through faith
> in Jesus Christ to all who believe. There
> is no difference, for all have sinned and
> fall short of the glory of God, and are
> justified freely by his grace through the
> redemption that came by Christ Jesus. God
> presented him in sacrifice of atonement,
> through faith in his blood.

Romans 3:21-25

The payoff of faith in Christ from Saint Paul's perspective was eternal life. It seems ironic that this is precisely what Hindus wish to avoid, but for Saint Paul it was a different kind of eternal life than that of continuous rebirth. One who was saved would go when he dies to be with God and Christ. Then, on the day of judgment when Christ is to come again, the faithful would receive new bodies and eternal life in a new creation that doesn't have the shortcomings of this one. Here is what Paul said about this:

> For the trumpet will sound, the dead
> will be raised imperishable, and we
> will be changed. For the perishable
> must clothe itself with the imperishable,
> and the mortal with immortality. When
> the perishable has been clothed with the
> imperishable, and the mortal with immortality,
> then the saying that is written will come
> true: "Death has been swallowed up in
> victory."
>   "Where, O death, is your victory?
>   "Where, O death, is your sting?"

1 Corinthians 15:52-55

One has to wonder, though, whether Jesus himself believed it was necessary to die and wait for the second coming to enter the kingdom of God. Consider the following:

> And (Jesus) said to them, "I tell you
> the truth, some who are standing here will
> not taste death before they see the kingdom
> of God come with power."

Mark 9:1

He did, however, believe that he would come again and collect his followers from among the living and the dead:

> At that time men will see the Son of Man
> coming in clouds with great power and glory.
> And he will send his angels and gather his
> elect from the four winds, from the ends of
> the earth to the ends of the heavens.

Mark 13:26-27

Jesus also believed in hell:

> And if your eye causes you to sin, pluck it
> out. It is better for you to enter the kingdom
> of God with one eye than to have two eyes and
> be thrown into hell, where,
> 'their worm does not die
> and the fire is not quenched.'

Mark 9:47-48

According to biblical scholars Jesus was quoting the prophet Isaiah of the Old Testament to draw a picture of hell from Jerusalem's permanently smoldering refuse-tip in the valley of Hinnon (Gehenna) and from dead bodies gradually being eaten away by worms.[21]

Let us consider the possibility that our personality survives death instead of our waking up to find that we are God. What, we might wonder, was Paul's idea of the type of body a person would have?

Here is an excerpt from the same letter quoted earlier that Paul wrote to the Corinthians:

> If there is a natural body there is also
> a spiritual body. So it is written: 'The
> first man Adam became a living being'; the
> last Adam, a life-giving spirit. The spiritual
> did not come first, but the natural and after
> that the spiritual. The first man was of the
> dust of the earth, the second man from heaven.

1 Corinthians 15:45-47

Could Paul have been talking about a morphic field when he spoke of a spiritual body in addition to a natural (flesh and blood) body? After the flesh and blood body roams the earth, does the spiritual body continue on? If my experience with what I think was Philippe's ghost was more than a coincidence and hallucination, this may well be the case. This idea would certainly also seem to be supported by the near death experiences (NDEs) which have been reported and written about ad infinitum since Raymond Moody's book, *Life After Life,* was first published in 1975. According to a 1992 Gallup poll some 13 million people in the United States claim to have gone through the dark tunnel toward the light.[22]

Materialists have tried to explain NDEs by telling us people were experiencing some sort of process which takes place in the brain when we die. But not all scientists agree. Consider what one medical doctor wrote:

> The Light is the one element of the
> near-death experience that brain researchers
> can't even come close to explaining. The
> testimony of children is clear on this point:
> The Light is the key element of the NDE.

How can we scientifically explain this light after death? I do not know of any biochemical or psychological explanation for why we would experience a bright light as the final stage of bodily death.[23]

One of the main elements of the morphic field of a species is that it contains the entire memory of all the members that have gone before. This can be seen in the development of a human embryo, for example, as it evolves from a fish-like creature through the various stages until it reaches human form. This is how physical characteristics such as the long necks of giraffes are propagated. It is how instincts develop and are passed along. If the memories of a species continue, our individual memories must live on in some way after we die as well, whether intact in individual fields, or at minimum as part of the greater field of mankind.

Let us consider the possibility that our individual field will continue and take a look at NDEs in this light. For one thing, the idea of the unity of all things is often created or reinforced by the experience. Raymond Moody tells us in his book, *The Light Beyond,* that NDEers return with a sense that everything in the universe is connected. They don't always find this concept easy to define but most have new respect for nature and the world around them. To illustrate, Dr. Moody quotes a man he described as a hard-driving, no-nonsense businessman who had an NDE during a cardiac arrest at the age of sixty-two:

The first thing I saw when I awoke in the hospital was a flower, and I cried. Believe it or not, I had never really seen a flower until I came back from death. One big thing I learned when I died was that we are all part of one big, living universe. If we think we can hurt another person or another living thing without hurting ourselves, we are sadly mistaken. I look at a forest or a flower or a bird now, and say, "That is me, part of me." We are connected with all things and if we send love

60

along those connections, then we are happy.[24]

Five stages seem to be common to NDEs:

1. A sense of being dead; sudden awareness of a fatal accident or of not surviving an operation.
2. An out-of-body experience; the sensation of peering down on one's body. NDEers often report back the scene of their near-death with uncanny accuracy, quoting doctors and witnesses verbatim.
3. Some kind of tunnel experience, a sense of moving upward or through a narrow passage.
4. Light; light "beings"; God or a God-like entity. For those having a "hell-like" experience, the opposite may be true--darkness or a lack of light.
5. Life review; being shown one's life, sometimes high-lighting one's mistakes or omissions.[25]

An argument can be made that the NDE adheres fairly closely to the Christian idea of heaven and hell. Heaven is generally supposed to be a place or a state of being where one is with God or Christ. This corresponds to the Light and the beings of light described in stage four.

Hell is often thought of as being separated from God, or lost in the darkness so to speak. In her bestseller, *Embraced by the Light,* Betty Eadie writes, "Some who die as atheists, or those who have bonded to the world through greed, bodily appetites, or other earthly commitments find it difficult to move on, and they become earth-bound. They often lack the faith and power to reach for, or in some cases even to recognize, the energy and light that pulls us toward God. These spirits stay on the earth until they learn to accept the greater power around them and to let go of the world. When I was in the black mass (of the tunnel) before moving towards the light, I felt the presence of such lingering spirits."[26]

The review that takes place in stage five also could be the judgment spoken of in the Bible, although it is not what most Christians are expecting since in NDEs judgment is made not by God or the Being of Light but by the very individual whose life is in review. Dr. Moody wrote of this:

> When the life review occurs, there are no more physical surroundings. In their place is a full color, three-dimensional, panoramic review of every single thing the NDEers have done in their lives.
>
> This usually takes place in a third-person perspective and doesn't occur in time as we know it. The closest description I've heard of it is that the person's whole life is there at once.
>
> In this situation, you not only see every action that you have ever done, but you also perceive immediately the effect of every single one of your actions upon the people in your life.
>
> So for instance, if I see myself doing an unloving act, then immediately I am in the consciousness of the person I did that act to, so that I feel their sadness, hurt, and regret.
>
> On the other hand, if I do a loving act to someone, then I am immediately in their place and I can feel the kind and happy feelings.
>
> Through all of this, the Being is with those people, asking them what good they have done with their lives. He helps them through this review and helps them put all the events of their life in perspective.
>
> All of the people who go through this come away believing that the most important thing in their life is love.
>
> For most of them, the second most important thing in life is knowledge. As they see life scenes in which they are learning things, the Being points out that one of the things they can take with them at death is knowledge. The other is love.[27]

This emphasis on the importance of love brings to mind the teachings of Christ and is echoed in the words of

Betty Eadie: "With all of this understanding, I understood again that love is supreme. Love must govern. Love always governs the spirit, and the spirit must be strengthened to rule the mind and flesh."[28]   She also wrote, "Whatever we become here in mortality is meaningless unless it is done for the benefit of others. Our gifts and talents are given to us to help us serve. And in serving others we grow spiritually."[29]

So, we have the field. We have the fields of species and we have the fields of individuals and all is constantly changing and evolving. Again, let us ask why? What is the purpose?

In his book, *The Seat of the Soul,* Gary Zukav argues that the purpose is the rounding out and eventual perfection of the soul. He wrote, "When the soul returns to its home, what has been accumulated in that lifetime is assessed with the loving assistance of its teachers and guides. The new lessons that have emerged to be learned, the new karmic obligations that must be paid, are seen. The experiences of the incarnation just completed are reviewed in the fullness of understanding. Its mysteries are mysteries no more. Their causes, their reasons, and their contributions to the evolution of the soul, and to the evolution of the souls with whom the soul shared its life, are revealed. What has been balanced, what has been learned, brings the soul ever closer to its healing, to its integration and wholeness."[30]

To which we must ask why? To what end?

If we think about this long and hard it will occur to us that perhaps the transcendent, the universal field, the "one life," has set about the task of duplicating itself. Think about it. As Richard Dawkins observed in his study of cheetahs and gazelles, propagation is an underlying theme of nature. Every organism from the smallest amoeba to the biggest whale has this as a primary objective. Why shouldn't the universe, the largest organism of them all? Perhaps at some point in our development, long after this particular life is finished, we will not only be the field, we will be a new field, a new reality.

A less grand view is that we will be fully-evolved beings within the field whose function is to help in the construction of new realities, new universes. This idea was held by the occultist, W. E. Butler. He said, "We're going to be universe builders in company with God. We are going to be tools, instruments in the hands of the Eternal as His will prevails in the universes which He has formed and in which He lives, moves and has His being and which He is bringing back to perfection from their fallen state. And you and I have the privilege of being coworkers with Him and with the whole of creation which is part of His work."[31]

W. E. Butler also said:

> The time will come when all physical life
> has gone, the inner planes have gone, and
> all that remains is the Eternal Spirit
> brooding over the creation that was and
> which has now reached its fruition, the
> fruits thereof absorbed within Itself.
> Then, in the far distant future, there
> will come a time in the dawn of the gods
> when the life of Kether flows once more,
> and Binah is reestablished; when the plastic
> substance of the universe again comes into
> manifestation. All the old forms, all the
> old knowledge of the Logos now locked up in
> that wallet which the fool of the tarot carries,
> all that knowledge will come into manifestation
> again. All the sons and daughters of the One
> Life who have evolved in this universe will
> return as universe builders. We shall be the
> morning stars who sing together for joy as we
> begin to work together in cooperation with the
> Logos in His new task in the new Universe in a
> realm of new ideals and new conceptions of
> reality.[32]

The question which immediately occurs is how can we be universe builders and the universe at the same time? Was Alan Watts wrong when he said that we would one day wake up and realize that we are God? Are the Hindus wrong about our ultimate reunification with Brahman?

I believe the likely explanation is that Watts, the Hindus, Jesus, Buddha and Butler are all correct in the same sense that Joseph Campbell said that all religions are true for their time.[33]   We are the universe. All of us are one and totally connected. At the same time we are cuttings from it. Metaphorically speaking we're the tree, but we're also a twig cut from it that is meant to grow into a new tree. If this is the case, and my money says it is, we have a long long way to go. Perhaps some of us will make it and others won't. What we don't want to have happen, you and I, is to end up as a couple of dinosaurs.

So let's get with it, which leads us back to the teachings of the Buddha. Rather than spend our time speculating on where things are headed we need to concentrate on the here and now. We need to ask ourselves how we can move closer to the ultimate goal in this lifetime. How can we enter Nirvana, or if you prefer another name, the kingdom of God? How can we become empowered? How can we be assured of eternal life?

The great religions tell us the way lies in subjugation of our egos, which means the relinquishing of self-centeredness, and in providing service of benefit to our fellow man. Gary Zukav wrote, "Before it incarnates, each soul enters into a sacred contract with the Universe to accomplish certain things. It enters into this commitment in the fullness of its being. Whatever the task that your soul has agreed to, all of the experiences of your life serve to awaken within you the memory of that contract, and to prepare you to fulfill it."[34]

In the next chapter we will begin to explore strategies for identifying our missions.

I sent my Soul through the Invisible, some letter of the Afterlife to spell, and by and by my Soul returned to me, and answered, I Myself and Heaven and Hell.

Omar Khayyam (?1048-?1122)

Chapter Three: Who Are You?

Did we incarnate and enter the physical realm with a specific mission or missions to accomplish as stated by Gary Zukav in the quotation at the end of the last chapter? If so, some aspect of ourselves would have to have existed before we were born. Let's examine this.

To the Materialist each individual human is an assembly of parts, the same as my twenty-three year old roadster. We are built of a brain, heart, blood vessels and muscles. The roadster has fuel injectors, pistons, a crank shaft and valves. It was put together in a factory. We were assembled in the womb. Fortunately for the roadster I have taken care of it with the result that it has outlasted many of its contemporaries and enjoyed a relatively good existence for a car. Humans seem to be subject to the same whims of capricious fate. One may be lucky and be born a Rockefeller or a Kennedy. Unlucky and enter the world in Somalia or some other Third World nation where living conditions are miserable and opportunities for a good life largely non-existent.

Or is it luck? We know from our studies that a human being is not an assembly of parts but rather a creation of the field; not a sum of individual pieces but a unified whole. His body's abilities were shaped by the evolution and experiences of his species in an unbroken chain dating to the first life on earth. He is a separate entity to the extent that he identifies himself as such, and on a deeper level totally at one with the field from which he sprang. Indeed, as he grows spiritually and moves through the stages described in the introduction, he will come to sense his connectedness to all of creation provided he advances far enough. He even may have a sudden insight, an epiphany, as did the woman in Chapter One when she was a child on the Pangbourne Moors. As the person who has experienced this insight grows in wisdom, experiences life, and moves into and through middle age, it will begin to dawn on her that the idea of fate as whimsical and arbitrary is contrary to personal experience. The nineteenth century German philosopher Arthur Schopenhauer observed in one of his essays, for example, that when an individual reaches an advanced age and looks back over his or her lifetime it seems to have followed a consistent plan as though composed by a master storyteller or novelist. Specific events and the meeting of individuals which seemed at the time to have come about by chance turn out to have been essential components in a constant storyline.

If this is so, and my personal experience says it is, we are compelled to ask who wrote the story?

In twentieth century jargon Schopenhauer would have said that it was an individual's subconscious mind. He would note that our dreams are composed by part of us of which we are unaware and would argue that our whole life is created by an unconscious aspect of ourselves which he labeled the *will within*. This *will within* coordinates with that of others so that the whole of human existence comes together like a symphony. Schopenhauer said that it is as though one dreamer were dreaming a giant dream in which each of the characters in the dream has his own individual dream.[1]

It appears Carl Jung was correct. We are all connected by what he called the collective unconscious. From what we have seen of the universal field there is only one mind, one organism, of which each of us is an aspect. Perhaps this is what John Donne had in mind 400 years ago when he said, "No man is an island." Our lives are intertwined. As a piece of the continent of mankind we have roles to play which affect other parts of the main. An individual we meet apparently by chance becomes a key player in the story of our life just as in turn we play key roles in the lives of others whether or not we realize it when it happens.

Let us now ask, what is the part of us, our personal puppeteer, who compels us to play our different roles at different times in the giant dream of humanity? Where did this unconscious aspect of ourselves come from? Why aren't we aware of it? Was it created at the moment the egg, the sperm and the morphic fields of our mother and father united? Or did it develop as our egos developed, a sort of parallel construction on an unconscious level?

We have seen that a morphic field contains the entire memory of a species. In a giraffe this becomes manifest in the shape of its neck and the instincts it is born with. Why would the morphic field of a human be different? In at least a general sense we are born with the memory of every human being and prehuman creature that came before. We also are connected to the mind of every other human through the medium of the field. These two aspects of us remain unconscious, however, unless we happen to be clairvoyant or, perhaps, schizophrenic. (We no doubt quickly would become the latter if they did not remain so.)

All right, you say. But unconscious memories and subconscious psychic connections do not account for the hidden puppeteer, the aspect of myself which quietly tells me I'm making a mistake when I let my ego lead me into trouble. Perhaps you, too, have made or were about to make a decision based on some ego demand or urge, the part of us that becomes afraid, that lusts, that rationalizes, that worries what others will think. Something inside said you would live to regret the decision if you followed through. At that moment you were in touch, however briefly, with your higher self, the aspect of you which is in touch and in tune with the big dream and the Big Dreamer.

When we get off the track of the dream, things go awry. Our life gets messy. Perhaps you know someone as I do who married a person he knew deep down he was going to divorce. Unfortunately the feeling didn't poke through into conscious awareness until the day the invitations were mailed. Even so, there was still time to call it off. Two years later, after he and his bride had split, he came to the realization he'd (his ego had) talked himself into going through with the marriage because he didn't have the courage to tell the girl or his friends and his parents and her parents that the marriage would be a mistake. He should have listened to the choreographer of his dream but he did not and lived through a nightmare as a result.

Elisabeth Kübler-Ross, the Swiss born physician and author of the perennial best-seller *On Death and Dying,* has been in attendance and helped to ease the deaths of thousands of patients, and she has studied the near death experiences of many thousands more. She has spoken of her own mystical, out of body experience[2] and is generally accepted as one of the world's leading authorities in these areas. In the process of her life and studies she has come to the conclusion that this inner voice is very real. In a lecture given in 1977 in San Diego and published the same summer in the *Co-Evolution Quarterly* she said, "If you listen to your inner voice, your inner wisdom--which is far greater than anybody else's as far as you are concerned--you will not go wrong and you will know what to do with your life."[3] It is too bad my friend had not been exposed to these words, or if he had, that he did not heed them.

We're back to the question, where did this puppeteer come from? Is he a parallel construction to the ego? Or is he built into the morphic field of a human being? Could it be that a higher self simply comes with being human the way a set of instincts are built into the morphic field of a giraffe? Perhaps. But this puppeteer, which I will from now on call the higher self or soul, seems so much more advanced than our ego. How could it have developed during the same short period of time? And why or how would it have developed without our knowing it? After all, the higher self knows the big picture, knows the dream. It realizes when we're about to make a mistake. Life would be so much easier if we could be in touch with this aspect of ourselves all the time instead of only in brief glimpses. But we usually are not in touch, at least not until we become enlightened.

Enlightened? That is correct. Once we move into that state of Nirvana, the Kingdom of God, that condition of knowing and sensing our connectedness on a gut level, our ego or lower self comes into harmony with our higher self or soul. This cannot help but happen and when it does we experience the major payoff of our struggle upward on the spiritual path: a life where the pieces fit, where we understand why we are here, our purpose and how we are to achieve it. Fear vanishes. We become patient, collected, serene. We are able to live in the eternal now and perhaps for the first time, truly experience and enjoy our life in the physical world.

We all know we have an ego. It is that part of our consciousness which has developed in this lifetime from an unfocused awareness in our early days in the crib to the consciousness that contains the memories of this life. It is the part of us that tells us we are separate from the rest of creation rather than a part of it. It is our personal identity. The self that worries, that fights for life, for achievement, for glory and for recognition. In contrast, the higher self or soul is not concerned with the trappings of the physical world. It seems to have been around for a long long time, perhaps since the epoch of mankind's evolution from a species driven by instinct into a species characterized by self awareness and free will. It may have been around even longer. It does not experience fear or worry but appears to believe it will continue to exist throughout eternity. It possesses no desire whatsoever for self-aggrandizement.

Wait. Did I say our first incarnation as a human? Yes. The evidence for reincarnation is too compelling to dismiss. Readers who are Christians may be put off by this or dismiss it out of hand because reincarnation generally is

71

not part of their theology. Nevertheless some scholars think that as the canon of the Church was formalized in the fourth and fifth centuries the concept of reincarnation was judged to be counterproductive since it was thought that some potential converts would resist or delay their acceptance of Christ because they would believe they'd have other chances in future lives. Reincarnation was eliminated as a result. Close scrutiny of the Bible will reveal, however, that Jesus and the followers of his day may have accepted it as fact. John the Baptist was supposed by some, for example, to be the prophet Elijah reincarnated. Jesus himself proclaimed this (in Matthew 11:14). Also, consider the story of Jesus healing the blind man as recounted in John 9:1-12, which begins as follows:

> As he went along, he saw a man blind
> from birth. His disciples asked him, 'Rabbi,
> who sinned, this man or his parents, that he
> was born blind?'
> 'Neither this man nor his parents
> sinned,' said Jesus, 'but this happened
> so that the work of God might be displayed
> in his life.'

Since the man was blind from birth, the only way his own sins could have caused his blindness was for him to have sinned in a former life. Jesus did not tell his followers this wasn't possible. To the contrary he seems to have assumed it was. (Though he gives another reason.)

In researching reincarnation I found that the libraries I frequent are well stocked in the subject. One of the best known and most cited works is that of University of Virginia professor Ian Stevenson called *Twenty Cases Suggestive of Reincarnation*. He studied hundreds of instances, mostly among children who remembered their most recent past life, and was careful to include only those he could document, cases where the subject knew information Stevenson could verify such as names and addresses and specific events.[4]

I'll spare you the details. You can probably find a

copy in your public library. Instead I will give you a quick summary of the most amazing and instructive account of reincarnation I know about. It was reported in the 1988 book, *Many Lives, Many Masters.* The author, Brian L. Weiss, M.D., is no loony tune. He is a Phi Beta Kappa, magna cum laude graduate of Columbia University who received his medical degree from Yale, interned at New York's Bellevue Medical Center and went on to become chief resident of the department of psychiatry at the Yale University School of Medicine. At the time of the case covered in his book he was head of the department of psychiatry at Mount Sinai Medical Center in Miami Beach.

Weiss is a medical doctor and a scientist who has published widely in professional journals. He was himself a skeptic who had no interest in reincarnation before the situation you will soon read about dropped into his lap. He was fully aware that colleagues in the field look askance at such things and waited six years before he gave into the feeling that he had an obligation to share what happened. He had much more to lose than to gain by telling the story of the woman called Catherine (not her real name) who came to him in 1980 seeking help for her anxiety, panic attacks and phobias. Read his book for yourself. I will hit only a few of the highlights here.

For eighteen months he used conventional therapy, which means he and Catherine talked about and analyzed her life and her relationships. When nothing worked he tried hypnosis in an effort to find out what she might be repressing which would account for her neuroses. Forgotten events in her childhood were in fact revealed which seemed to be at the root of several of her problems. As is customary in this type of therapy she was instructed to remember them and then brought out of the hypnotic state. Dr. Weiss discussed with her what had been uncovered in an effort to dispel her anxieties. But as days went by her symptoms remained as severe as ever.

He tried hypnotism again. This time he regressed her all the way to the age of two, but she recalled nothing that shed new light on her problems. He gave her firm instructions, "Go back to the time from which your symptoms arise."[5]   Nothing had prepared him for what happened next. She slipped into a past life that took place almost 4,000 years ago.   Weiss was astounded as she described herself, her surroundings and others in that particular life in detail including episodes, and in later sessions entire lifetimes, which seemed to be the root causes of problems. In all she said she had lived 86 times.

Weiss continued using the technique of hypnosis in an effort to rid Catherine of her neuroses. In once a week sessions which spanned a period of several months she recalled and recounted in detail the highlights of twelve previous lifetimes, including the moment of death in each. People who played a role in one often reappeared as someone else in another, including Dr. Weiss himself who had been her teacher some 3500 years ago.

Catherine had not had a happy existence over the last forty centuries. The overwhelming number of memories from her past lives were unhappy and proved to be the roots of her present day symptoms. As amazing as it may seem to to someone who discounts the possibility of multiple lifetimes, bringing them into her consciousness and talking about them enabled her to recover. Considering the number and intensity of her neuroses, psychotherapy normally would have lasted years before she was cured.   Her symptoms disappeared within a few months. She became happier and more at peace than she had ever been.

Weiss does not offer a scientific explanation for what happened. He now believes it is possible that part of her subconscious mind stored actual past-life memories. He also concedes that she may have tapped into what Carl Jung called the collective unconscious.[6]   But no matter which explanation is correct, he is convinced she was not faking. Weiss is an experienced psychotherapist. Catherine was unsophisticated and of average intelligence, a young woman who made her living as a laboratory technician. He thinks it impossible she could have pulled off such an elaborate hoax and kept it up every week for months. Think about it. She was a physically attractive twenty-eight year old woman of average intelligence. She had a high school degree and some vocational training. Could she have faked her neuroses? Could she have faked gradual improvement from one visit to the next all the way to a state of being completely free of them? It hardly seems likely. Also, and this is where the plot thickens, she conveyed information about Weiss's father and an infant son, both of whom had died. Weiss is convinced she could not have known anything about them through normal channels.

This message from the other side leads to what is most amazing about her story: the spaces between past lives. Once, after having been murdered, she floated out of her body and was reborn very quickly. At the end of her next life she described an experience remarkably similar to that related by thousands who have been clinically dead and come back to life. She rose out of her body, felt at peace and was aware of an energy-giving light. It was at this time in this session that spirit entities spoke through her to Dr. Weiss for the first time. In a loud, husky voice and without hesitation Catherine said, "Our task is to learn, to become God-like through knowledge. We know so little. You are here to be my teacher. I have so much to learn. By knowledge we approach God, and then we can rest. Then we come back and help others."[7]

Although Catherine was able to recall her past lives after she was brought out of a hypnotic state, she was never able to recall, nor was she particularly interested in remembering the conversations Dr. Weiss had through her with several different spirit entities. These "masters" as he came to call them spoke through her primarily for his benefit and only indirectly for hers. I will not go into detail about these exchanges. You can read this book for yourself. Essentially, they told him that we incarnate into the physical world to learn what cannot be learned on the nonphysical planes. In that realm whatever is felt or imagined instantly appears real or greatly magnified. The slightest ill will toward someone becomes rage. The smallest feeling of affection turns to all encompassing love. If you imagine a demon, a thought form of it suddenly will be before you. If you picture in your mind a lovely sunset viewed from a secluded beach, you will believe that you are there. It is because of this that we need the thickness of matter. Matter slows things down so we can work them out. The earth is a school. The most important things we come here to learn are charity, hope, faith and love, as well as to trust and not to have fear.

I will not dwell on the case reported by Dr. Weiss. While I will refer back to it later, I now will take the balance of this chapter to give you food for thought about the workings of reincarnation. I must admit that some of what you are about to read at first seemed as fantastic to me as it no doubt will to you. Nevertheless, like Dr. Weiss, I feel compelled to share at least some of what I have learned.

As we have seen, underlying and supporting the physical plane is a totally interconnected and invisible field. This field is the life force or the Big Dreamer and it is true to say that the entire universe is one big organism, parts of which have become differentiated to a greater or lesser extent. These parts range from you and me to the trees and flowers to planets and moons to rocks and pebbles. When the life force is withdrawn from anything, be it an animal, plant, person or object, the life force continues to exist but the object it supported no longer is animated by it. That thing ceases to be alive (informed by the life force) and turns to dust. This is true of what we normally consider living things (plants and animals) and it is true of what we may have thought until now were inanimate objects (rocks, moons, mountains). Although the process of decay and return to dust takes longer for the latter, it will nonetheless happen in time when the life force is no longer present.

As Claire DuMond came to know in my novel, *Out of Body, Into Mind,* the secret of life is the urge to become. It is an impetus to evolve into a separate entity, one that eventually will become aware of itself. We all are souls. Some may have started out as an undifferentiated part of the field and evolved into a pattern (a morphic field) through experience with the physical realm. When a soul has learned all it can in one form it seeks a new experience that will allow it to continue its upward push. Ultimately, it will grow and develop until it reaches the perfected state from which it became separated long ago.

We live in a multi-dimensional reality, although under normal circumstances our physical senses allow us to experience only height, width and depth. Souls are evolving in other dimensions and they are evolving on other planets in other solar systems of this universe. Your soul could have come from elsewhere and now is continuing its journey here. It could be much older than life on earth. While recognizing this may be the case, one view of how souls evolved along with life on this planet will be presented in the paragraphs that follow. (This is not the last word on the subject and is meant only to give you an inkling of how the process works. A full treatment easily could fill an entire book and may be the topic of my next.)

A theory accepted by some followers of eastern religions is that souls which began their journeys here have been around in some form since the beginning of life on earth but did not become differentiated until the epoch recounted in the myth of Adam and Eve. (Scientists would probably estimate this to have occurred about 100,000 years ago.) A splitting off or separation from the field came about which resulted in self awareness and free will. These souls would have followed the course of evolution from one-celled animals in the sea, to creatures who first walked on land, to tiny mammals, to apes, to *Homo Sapiens*.

Others believe that souls evolved out of the mineral kingdom, then moved into the lower forms of the vegetable kingdom, and after many growing seasons into the higher forms of the vegetable kingdom. They believe this took thousands of years, but that it was only at the next level when they passed from the vegetable to the animal kingdom that any sort of division came about. At this stage there was still no individual higher self or soul but merely a group consciousness or group soul that was common to all of the animals of the same species. You may recall that colonies of insects, schools of fish and flocks of birds have a single morphic field or in effect a single group soul. This is similar to what would have been experienced. (The life force or group souls of insects, fish and birds are on a different path, however, than that being followed by a human soul. An explanation of this path is beyond the scope of this book.)

A Soul beginning its sojourn in the animal kingdom would have started at the bottom, proceeded to worm-like creatures and so on up the ladder to wild animals. Much would have been learned along the way, the lessons of self preservation and the need to work in order to survive, for example. Obtaining food would have been a daily chore which could never have been forsaken. As climates changed or food became scarce, souls would have learned to adapt or to look for new sources. Thus the basic survival lessons of the animal kingdom would have been internalized. Maternal instincts also would have been developed during this time in a soul's evolution, according to this theory.

Proponents of this scenario believe that during lifetimes as the group souls of wild animals these souls might have come to fear man because of his cruelty toward them. Only after animals became domesticated and souls experienced this form did they come to trust humans. They hold that trusting humans is a basic requisite for evolving into the soul of a human and maintain that a soul which incarnated as the group soul of a herd of cattle or sheep eventually would progress into a collection of cats, horses or dogs. As a soul grew more manlike through repeated incarnations, as its trust in humans grew and the bonds between its species and humans became stronger, the number of individuals comprising the group soul would have become less and less with each succeeding incarnation. Eventually the soul would incarnate as perhaps two very human-like horses or dogs or other animal which is a close companion to man. In its next incarnation the soul would make the leap into human form and become completely differentiated, have but one body, though still a long way to go in its push toward perfection.

The population of the world has exploded in recent decades. The theory outlined above may be the course that was taken by only a small percentage of souls alive today. The truth is souls are pouring into this world from all over the place. The implications are obvious. If we are born in the United States we come into the world with equal rights under the law but we are all far from equal in the mental department.

Let us consider the process of evolution of a human soul. When a new soul starts his human lives the number of foolish or evil actions, thoughts and words he is responsible for far exceeds those of the good variety. This is understandable. It is also where the law of karma comes into play, which is a basic learning tool. Like Newton's law, this one says that for every action there is an equal and opposite reaction except that, in this case, every thought, word or deed must produce a definite result, good or bad, and that result must be worked out by us in our lives at the physical level. This is one of the ways we learn and one reason why many lives at the physical level sometimes are necessary. The Bible tells us, "As you sow, so shall you reap," or as an old friend of mine in the ad business was often heard to say, "What goes around comes around."

A selfish act on your part which causes misery to someone else earns a unit of bad karma that must be repaid by your suffering from a similar action at the hand of another, either in this lifetime or in one to come. A kind act on your part means that a unit of good karma has been earned, the result of which can be either the erasing of a unit of bad karma or the gift of the same amount of kindness from someone else.

When I first learned about this and the truth of it settled in, I began to think back over my life and to remember things I had done to others which had caused them pain. A number of instances of thoughtlessness and two or three of outright cruelty came to mind. I truly felt remorse and was thrown into a kind of depression. It was as though a black cloud hung over me and my future. I could almost feel the pain I had caused and shall never forget wondering how I would ever repay these debts. At that time I did not know the therapeutic and practical value of confessing my sins directly to God or to Christ and asking forgiveness. (This will be discussed in a later chapter.) Rather, I was convinced I was doomed to suffer the same amount of misery I had inflicted. This played heavily on me until one day I was running along the Canal of Burgundy during one of my summer sojourns to France and I came to a stop and said, "Please, God, Please.   Even out the score. Give me a level playing field. Make whatever needs to take place happen so that these debts are wiped clean."

I emphatically do not advise you to do this. Sometimes one gets exactly what one asks for. In this case it came three days later when I was back in the States and took my daughter's brand new ten speed bike for a test spin down the hill in front of our house. My foot slipped, caught on the pavement and my Achilles tendon was severed by the metal pedal. The result was a ghastly wound. I spent almost two weeks in the hospital, had two operations, suffered a great deal of physical pain, and was in a cast from the tip of my toe to the top of my thigh for eight weeks. It took nine months before the wound was completely closed and another nine before I was able to walk without a limp. But this was not all that happened. While still in the cast, my wife announced she was leaving me, filing for divorce and taking my only child with her to live in France.

It was not a good year, but at least the slate was wiped clean. I also developed spiritually. (This is always characteristic of the answer to a prayer as we will see later.) Another important thing the experience taught is that it is possible to get in touch with your personal teachers and guides. I do not advise you to follow the same course, however, because I'm not sure the process has to be quite as difficult as what I experienced.

Let's think for a moment about the new soul who goes about creating much more havoc than I ever dreamed of in my youth. Fortunately for him no man is expected to suffer more in one lifetime than he can stand. The units of bad karma made by him in the early lives which aren't worked off by good deeds or a poke in the mouth are carried forward for working out in future lives.

A person with a young soul appears to have very little if any conscience. He simply can't hear the still small voice. (Jiminy Cricket can't seem to get through.) The result is that during the early incarnations a person is likely to pile up more debt than he works off. But as time goes by and he continues to incarnate, the connection grows between the place where his conscience is housed, his higher self which is eternal, and his ego which must be built up from scratch each time around. Once the lines of communication begin to open conditions start to improve. At last the right wavelength is found and the mother ship comes in loud and clear. This is why a person with an old soul (one that is more experienced) appears to have a highly developed sense of right and wrong. When this happens the bad karma stored up from early lives is whittled down each time around.

Now we're going to get into information few people know anything about. In the evolution of the soul from a savage to a perfect state, human beings use three vehicles of consciousness. I will call these: 1.) the mental or mind body, 2.) the astral or emotional body, and 3.) the physical body. (The latter is the one I hope you are in right now and in which I definitely am enclosed as I pound the keyboard. Otherwise, you're going to have difficulty turning pages.)

These three bodies are used by us when functioning in three different states of consciousness, which are: the mental plane, the astral plane, and the physical plane. The home of the soul around which these bodies are drawn is the upper part of the mental plane, which I will call the causal level. It is from here that the great dream is choreographed and from here that your personal puppeteer pulls your strings. It is also from this level that we enter each incarnation.

We don't exit physical life onto this level, however. When the time comes to leave the physical world behind we do so by passing onto the astral plane. This is where people generally go who have NDEs or other out-of-body experiences. Most will think they've reached heaven or hell, but it is in fact a kind of purgatory. They've arrived in a place where the evolution which began in the life just lived is continued. It is here they will be received by beings of light, for throughout a life in the physical world and at key points as we evolve in the nonphysical realm as well, we are aided by guides or "masters" such as those who spoke to Dr. Weiss through Catherine. These masters had human experiences like ourselves and are now much more evolved. They have arrived at a point where they have no further need to incarnate. Dr. Kübler-Ross assures us everyone has them and that many children are able to see and communicate with these entities which she refers to as guardian angels. They are the "imaginary" playmates many have but seem to "lose" by the time they start school, perhaps because their parents tell them they are now too old for such things. Dr. Kübler-Ross spoke of this in one of her lectures, telling the audience that when a person is dying they may get back in touch with the childhood friend.

"There he is again," one old lady said. Kübler-Ross asked who. "You must know, when I was a little kid he used to always be around me. But I have totally forgotten that he existed." A day later the woman died, happy in the knowledge that someone who loved her was waiting.[8]

As a result of my efforts to communicate with my personal spiritual guides I have come to believe that there are seven of them. You may have more or fewer depending on what you're on earth to accomplish. (I wish I had one who could spell, but fortunately my computer now helps me with that.)

Something I find interesting is how frequently the number seven recurs in matters of spiritual growth. For example I understand there to be seven levels of the astral plane. This was revealed to me before I read Dr. Weiss's book. Yet in that book one of the masters says there are seven planes in the nonphysical realm: "There are seven planes in all, seven planes, each one consisting of many levels, one of them being the plane of recollection. On that plane you are allowed to collect your thoughts. You are allowed to see your life that has just passed."[9] I must admit that this is similar to but not precisely the information I've been given. My understanding is that there are seven levels of the astral plane and seven of the mental and that each one of these planes is as vast and varied as the physical plane we now inhabit. In effect this makes fourteen planes with "many levels" if you want to look at it that way, but I'm not going to argue points such as these. In my opinion details of this nature are unimportant. What is important is to understand that the nonphysical realm, your natural home, is vast by comparison to this world we now inhabit. What intrigues me is the recurrence of the number seven. For example, the development of a human from childhood to old age is a stair step affair divided roughly into periods of seven years. We go through life transitions about at the ages of seven, fourteen, twenty-one, twenty-eight, thirty-five and so on. I first read about this fifteen or more years ago in Gail Sheely's book, *Passages*, and it certainly has been the case for me personally.

No matter how many levels there may be, whether they are called astral and mental planes or some other term is used, a soul on its journey through the nonphysical on its way back to the physical does not have to spend time on each and every one. Following an incarnation and a stop on the "plane of recollection" (level two of the astral), a soul will arrive on the astral level that accords with how far he has come in his personal evolution. A person is still operating with his earthly ego at this point. As he continues to learn and evolve he will work his way from the level he arrived on to perhaps the next one up. Eventually, he will experience what some believe to be similar to a second death. This is in fact a journey from the astral world to the mental world and entirely painless, a simple dropping of the astral body so that only the mental one is left. Before we incarnate again, we will go through what some describe as a third death, a dropping of the mental body. Others would argue that it might be more accurate to say this is a full incorporation of the mental body into the soul. Whichever is the case, all that will be left is the soul.

As with everything there are exceptions. Perhaps not each of us passed from the astral plane to the mental plane and lost our astral and mental bodies before incarnating this time. When a life is cut short, the path through the nonphysical may be short-circuited, too. We are meant to accomplish certain things, learn certain lessons in each incarnation and if we don't, particularly if we die prematurely, we may come back very quickly for another go. This seems to be what happened the time Catherine was murdered. Under hypnosis she recalled the sensation of floating from her body, spending a brief time and then being born again. This also may be what is seen in cases reported by Ian Stevenson among children who died in their previous life as a child and shortly were born again. Perhaps they remembered who they were before because they had not journeyed through the astral and mental planes. Maybe their memories were still fresh, not having spent much time on the other side or having passed through all the normal steps.

We each come into a life to face and overcome certain problems or to work out karma from a previous incarnation. This is why suicide is seldom a solution to a person's difficulties. If we kill ourselves to avoid them we will have to come back and face a similar situation again. Not only are we wasting time, we actually may create additional negative karma because of the grief we cause others as a result of taking our own life. This adds to what will have to be worked out in a future life.

Let's examine what happens on the astral plane, the realm where we arrive immediately following physical death. The first level is a state of consciousness where we can still view the physical plane, and we will arrive here if we have some reason or desire to do so as was the case with Philippe in Marseille. A great deal of refinement or improvement can take place here for those who still have much to learn. For example, let's imagine a character like the Scrooge of Charles Dickens who loves money for its own sake. During his life he took great pleasure in counting the gold coins and calculating how much more wealth he had than his neighbor. From his new vantage point he still will be able to see the wealth he left behind and watch what happens to it. Imagine his sorrow when his good-for-nothing relatives pick apart his estate and squander his horde. He indeed may suffer, but no one but himself is punishing him. He now will have the time and opportunity to reflect about the true value of money and to learn the lesson that he must get away from attachments to physical things if he is to find true and lasting happiness.

Another case might be the extremely jealous person who thinks he is in love with someone when in reality all he wants is to possess that individual, body and soul, for his own gratification. A man who truly loves his wife or girlfriend would be happy and thankful when his dearly departed becomes the object of the affections of others. But if he was jealous in life he will remain so after death and go through the torture of watching others move in on what he considered his private territory. This man's spiritual guides surely will point out how foolish he is but he must come to realize this on his own. He must learn that to achieve a state of peace he must eliminate selfishness from his love. He must come to know that no one can own another. As the saying goes, "What we give we keep. What we keep we lose." We can't even own a physical object or money. Think about it. Your house or your car aren't things you own in the sense that you can possess them forever. You only borrow them for awhile during the time you're here on earth.

Many who die will spend almost no time at all on the first level of the astral plane for they have no need or reason to. Let's move on to a discussion of the next. It is here that the panoramic review takes place described so nicely by Raymond Moody. I will not go into this at any length since it was already covered in some detail in Chapter Two (pages 61-62). Essentially we see each and every action or stance or attitude we took in our past life and the result, actually feeling as others felt at the time; experiencing their joy or anguish. Our guide or guides are present here to help us interpret the meaning of our life and to learn from it. It is difficult to imagine what someone like a Hitler would experience but it certainly would be no less than the worst hell imaginable, although no one but himself would be punishing him. The review is a learning experience resulting from an individual's own actions. No doubt the more advanced one is spiritually the more he or she will benefit.

After the review is complete some will choose to remain at this second level and others, the more advanced, will move on. This astral sphere has the look and feel of the physical realm and is similar in many respects. Most people live in houses or apartments in cities or in towns. They go shopping, tend their gardens and play pinochle with friends. Here they make their conditions by the projection of their thoughts. If one expected to be in heaven, he will get what he expected heaven to be. If he thinks he belongs in hell, and my guess is few people do, he will have the hell he envisioned. If he thinks he should have the best, he will get his idea of whatever that is. If he thinks he deserves less, less is his. In this way the second level is like the earth because the same is true here whether or not a person realizes it. The big difference is, on the astral plane a thought instantly becomes a person's reality, whereas consciously projecting one's thoughts into reality on the physical plane is a challenge. It takes a while.

Projecting our *unconscious* thoughts into reality is a snap, though, isn't it? Just look around. The line from Proverbs in the Old Testament, "As a man thinketh in his heart, so is he," embraces the whole of our being down to every condition and circumstance of life. This is the lesson of the second level. Once people learn it, most of them will get bored. How much fun would it be to put together a complicated business deal, for example, work hard to out maneuver the other guy, only to find out all you have to do to get a signed contract is imagine doing so? Want to win at poker? Land on double zero in roulette? No sweat, just think. In a world such as this your team would go to the Super Bowl every single year. And win. Boring.

It is the third and fourth levels where things start to get interesting provided you're into intellectual pursuits. Institutions are to be found where one can learn or refine creative skills such as painting and music. If you want to know about medicine or archaeology, this is the place. Name your interest. It's like having the best schools and universities at your disposal. All you have to do is pick a subject.

The fifth and sixth levels are where what might be compared to graduate schools of universities or research and development departments at companies are found. Individuals who have become experts in a particular disciple continue their research and, if they wish, exchange ideas and information with others in the field.

The seventh level of the astral plane is a transitional sphere which must be traversed in order to reach the mental world. It is a sort of way station on the trip back to the higher self or soul which remains always on the causal level (level seven) of the mental world. It is here that we will be rejoined by guides and assisted in a "second death." This process is painless and is in fact a shedding of the astral body so that all that remains surrounding the soul is the mental body.

The first sensation upon entering the mental world is a feeling of well-being and buoyant health; a profound sense of bliss or peace. This plane also has seven levels but as is the case with the astral, we need not and probably will not visit all of them. Each person will arrive on the one that corresponds to the vibrations of his spiritual and mental development. After a while he will realize he has entered another dimension and that others like himself exist here who can communicate and exchange information via the medium of thought.

It is in the dreamlike state of this sphere that what has been learned on the physical and astral planes is sorted out and consolidated. In the process this knowledge is added to the permanent reservoir already accumulated in previous lives. When this is complete, a person will proceed to the highest level of the mental plane, where some have called the "third death" or dropping of the mental body occurs. (Others describe it as a total incorporation.) What now remains is the permanent or eternal self, which I've called the higher self or soul, the entity which has been in existence ever since it individualized.

The time now has come to prepare to reenter the physical realm. With the help of guides the soul considers the qualities and characteristics it lacks and the experiences it needs to continue its evolution. The karma to be worked out must be taken into account and coordination undertaken with other souls to whom debts are owed. Cohorts from previous lives also are evolving as they proceed from one life to another. Bonds may have been formed, either through love or hate or something left unresolved, that will bring them back together. For example, Dr. Weiss learned from the masters that the infant son who died had been in reality a highly advanced soul whom he and his wife had known in previous lives. This person had completed his incarnations on the physical plane but chose to come back a final time so that the karmic debts of his friends (Dr. Weiss and his wife) could be settled. The child was born with an abnormal heart and lived only a few weeks. Nonetheless his brief life had a profound effect in several ways, not the least of which was to influence the choice by Dr. Weiss of which medical specialty to pursue.[10]

Each incarnation is planned much as a writer might outline or prepare the plot skeleton of a novel. The elements must be in place and the supporting characters ready and waiting. Perhaps most important, the proper parents must be chosen. This can be a difficult and tricky task for the advanced soul since the possibilities are limited. Race, nation, region and familial circumstances are factors. For example, someone who was a bigot in their past lifetime may come back clothed in the race they were prejudiced against so as to experience the other end of the stick and work out the karma they created.

Once the details are complete the time comes for the soul to begin its descent to rebirth. Their are several theories of how this takes place. One holds that the soul brings around it a new mental body; another that the mental body has never departed and is immanent in the aura of the soul. Whatever the case, the mental facility in this incarnation will be a better vehicle of consciousness than the last because it will include on a latent level the results of mental efforts in the past incarnation.

Next an astral body is needed. This one also will be better that the last because it will embody emotional progress made in the past physical life and the work done on the astral plane. If for example music became a passion and one studied it, the person may have an urge to take this up in the life to come, either as a profession or for relaxation. The development of musical talent will come easily as a result.

Finally, the soul wants a physical body. This might be compared to an overcoat in that it is not necessarily reflective of what is inside and is acquired by being born into a family in the conventional way. It will have the genetic and morphic imprints of that family. Unlike the two bodies within, it may or may not be better than that of the previous incarnation. Much depends on the lessons to be learned in the new life. The body one gets will be the body one needs.

Now a new persona is on its way, sent out from the mother ship of the soul like a knight to the crusades. It has missions to accomplish and guides along side to help. A new ego will begin to form as soon as the baby looks up from his crib and begins making an effort to bring its surroundings into focus.

Most of us who have been around babies and small children instinctively know that they have just arrived from some heavenly place. I can see this clearly in my daughter, Hannah Grace, who at this writing has just turned one year old. The quality I'm thinking about is one that has been recognized by poets down through the centuries and was best captured, I believe, by William Wordsworth in the fifth stanza of his poem "Ode." (The subtitle is, "Intimations of Immortality from Recollections from Early Childhood.")

> Our birth is but a sleep and a forgetting:
> The Soul that rises with us, our life's Star,
>   Hath had elsewhere its setting,
>   And cometh from afar:
> Not in entire forgetfulness,
> And not in utter nakedness,
> But trailing clouds of glory do we come
>   From God, who is our home:
> Heaven lies about us in our infancy!
> Shades of the prison-house begin to close
>   Upon the growing boy,
> But he beholds the light, and whence it flows,
>   He sees it in his joy;
> The Youth, who daily farther from the east
>   Must travel, still is Nature's Priest,
>   And by the vision splendid
>   Is on his way attended;
> At length the Man perceives it die away,
> And fade into the light of common day.

Whether this little person "trailing clouds of glory"

makes progress in this incarnation, whether she fulfills her destiny or slides backward, will depend in large measure on the efforts and abilities of her parents. Think for a moment how important it is that we create a loving environment in which she can flourish and develop and pursue "natural" talents. Indeed, we can make it easy for her or difficult and in the process create a good deal of negative or positive karma for ourselves. In a very real way our parents are our guides at least until we're grown. It is an awesome responsibility.

All that our invisible guides can do is provide us with guidance when it is sought and help create favorable conditions for us to "pursue our bliss," as Joseph Campbell called it many times. Of course, the higher self will remain on the causal level doing its best to keep the lines of communication open and to play its role of puppeteer. Each of us, however, is born with free will. We always have the option of going against what our intuition (or "better judgment") tells us and screwing up.

The point I've tried to make in this chapter is that you are a soul with a body, not a body with a soul. Perhaps you have made some mistakes in this life of yours so far. If so, take heart. It may not be too late to make a mid-course correction, especially now that you know you are the driver, not the vehicle.

In the next chapter we will look at ways of identifying our missions and getting in touch with our guides and higher self.

Chapter Four: Are You Carrying Excess Baggage?

The purpose of life in the physical world is the creation of a separate identity or ego that will eventually reunite with its higher self or soul, bringing experience and knowledge that will lift the soul closer to its goal of perfection. The density of matter provides an environment where we can learn the lessons that result from our attitudes and our actions. Nothing is lost in the many cycles of reincarnation. One retains the self-assurance that comes as a result of success, and the inner-strength and compassion that is born of sorrow. Even the results of the destructive experiences one suffers are brought forward into each new life as was the case with Catherine, Dr. Weiss's patient who was cured of her phobias and neuroses after recalling them under hypnosis. Under normal circumstances our power of recall cannot conjure up specific events, but their fruits are no less than the sum of our total personality.

An individual is traversing an evolutionary course that spans many lives and according to his actions and experiences is either retreating from his true nature as spirit or advancing toward the divine goal. Laws of nature are at work in our personal evolution which have not yet been recognized by science. From life to life one is followed by the good or the bad he has created. Working out karma should not be viewed as punishment but rather as an opportunity to learn lessons which must be internalized. Here, for example, is what James, a brother of Jesus wrote about this: "Consider it pure joy, my brothers, whenever you face trials of many kinds, because you know that the testing of your faith develops perseverance. Perseverance must finish its work so that you may be mature and complete, not lacking anything." (James 1:2-4.)

Elisabeth Kübler-Ross echoed this in a lecture given in 1977 when she said, "All the hardships that you face in life, all the trials and tribulations, all the nightmares and all the losses, most people view as a curse, as a punishment by God, as something negative. If you would only realize that nothing that comes to you is negative. I mean nothing. All the trials and tribulations, the greatest losses, things that make you say, 'If I had known about this I would never have been able to make it through,' are gifts to you. It's like somebody has to temper the iron. It is an opportunity that you are given to grow. This is the sole purpose of existence on this planet earth. You will not grow if you sit in a beautiful flower garden and somebody brings you gorgeous food on a silver platter. But you will grow if you are sick, if you are in pain, if you experience losses, and if you do not put your head in the sand but take the pain and learn to accept it not as a curse, or a punishment, but as a gift to you with a very, very specific purpose."[1]

What one gives out will come back. This is a basic lesson to be learned. Almost any Christian is aware of St. Paul's words, "A man reaps what he sows." (Galatians 6:7.) What may be a new idea is that the good we do may not come back until many lives hence and the suffering we endure here and now may be the outcome of some thoughtless act carried out lifetimes ago. Catherine and her current-life boyfriend were still in the throws of settling karma from a tumultuous relationship that went back more than a thousand years. Problems such as theirs must be resolved in the physical world because the results of our thoughts and intentions are instantaneous in the nonphysical realm. Matter is needed to slow things down.

We create our own reality, a fact which must be digested before we move onto higher levels of the astral planes. This is as true here on earth as it is on the flip side but not as apparent. This isn't a new discovery although few people seem to have grasped it. Back in the nineteenth century, in a little book called *As a Man Thinketh*, James Allen wrote, "The outer world of circumstance shapes itself to the inner world of thought, and both pleasant and unpleasant external conditions are factors which make for the ultimate good of the individual. As the reaper of his own harvest, man learns both by suffering and bliss." And on the following page he said, "Even at birth the soul comes to its own, and through every step of its earthly pilgrimage it attracts those combinations which reveal itself, which are the reflections of its own purity and impurity, its strength and weakness."[2] His observation is uncanny. It should prompt each of us to examine our circumstances for clues as to what we need to do to accomplish what was set out for us before we were born.

We can begin by examining the circumstances of our birth and the parents and family to whom we were born. Our soul chose them for one or more reasons.

One of my missions was to write this book. I wouldn't have had an interest in doing so it if I had been born to Stage Two Christians. I'd have gone on to become a typical skeptic and would probably just now be coming out of that stage. I had to start in a different place: with skeptical parents whom I now realize reflect the audience for what I have to say. (Except, as someone who has picked up this volume you are likely to have had an insight or epiphany about the underlying connectedness of all things.)

My father and my mother were in the advertising business, a business of words and ideas. I've had an interest in writing for as long as I can remember. They allowed me to develop in my own way and to "follow my bliss." In other words, the conditions were all in place. It has taken until the age of fifty for me to be ready because it has taken me this long to put the pieces together. Yet even this would not have happened if I hadn't come to realize I'm not alone in the endeavor. The truth is I'm a conduit. The guardian angels or guides spoken of by Dr. Kübler-Ross, have provided or led me to the information you read in the last chapter. My higher self, the part of me who is in touch with the big dream of life and the Big Dreamer, also has played a role. For as Jesus said, "Ask and it will be given to you; seek and you will find; knock and the door will be opened to you. For everyone who asks receives; he who seeks finds; and to him who knocks the door will be opened." (Matthew 7:7-8.) To this James later added, "If any of you lacks wisdom, he should ask God, who gives generously to all without finding fault, and it will be given to him." (James 1:5.) When you're following your destiny all you need do is ask for guidance and expect an answer. Then be attentive. One way or another the answer will come. The trick to recognizing it lies in cultivating the quality of discernment. As James said in the next verse, "But when he asks, he must believe and not doubt, because he who doubts is like a wave of the sea, blown and tossed by the wind."

I will discuss techniques later that you will be able to use to get in touch with your guides and your higher self. At that time I will ask, what is your bliss? What have you been interested in for as long as you can remember? How does this fit with the circumstances you were born into? Are you now doing what you like? Does what you do help others in some way? But first, there's likely to be some baggage you're carrying around that needs to be discarded. This baggage is what leads to the doubts James was talking about that may be causing you to be like "a wave of the sea, blown and tossed by the wind." It falls into the category of destructive attachments you may have, feelings of guilt about your own past actions, and underlying fears that have been programmed into you since birth (or before). You will be blocked from advancing toward enlightenment and you will not achieve your potential in this lifetime as long as you hold on to this junk, so it's time to clean out the attic.

Let's talk about destructive attachments. If you have

not done so the first thing I want to urge you to do is forgive. Forgive yourself and forgive others. Karma is created by your thoughts and this includes thoughts toward yourself.

If you are in an abusive relationship, get out of it. Get out of it and forgive the abuser. As long as you hold onto bitterness it will come back to you.

Perhaps your parents pushed you in a direction you didn't want to go. Maybe they abused you. Perhaps it all happened a long time ago. Yet it may still be having a negative effect on you. What possible good can it do to hold onto those feelings? You're creating a bond that eventually will have to be worked out if not in this lifetime, then another. Begin today to dissolve it.

Let me tell you a story that will show one way. Once I worked with a man who was the most unlovable person I have ever met. By this I mean that I found him very difficult to like. I saw him as mean and spiteful and petty. By a series of what seemed coincidences he became my partner in business, an advertising agency. He owned the largest share, over fifty percent, and ultimately was able to call all the shots. We disagreed at every turn. Not surprisingly, he unwittingly turned out to be one of my teachers.

About six months after we came together in business I traveled to New York to visit with the editors of *Ad Age* and *ADWEEK* and the ad columnist for the *New York Times* among others in an effort to drum up publicity for our little agency. I had breakfast meetings and lunch meetings and after-work-drink meetings and was dragged around from one place to another by our publicist who invariably gave me a splitting headache because she talked so much and so fast and was such a bundle of undirected energy. Some people would surely enjoy this sort of thing, but I'm basically an introverted and introspective man who prefers to sit by the fire and read a good book.

Nevertheless, on the morning I was back in my office in Richmond I thought I'd struck gold when I opened the *New York Times* to the business section and saw my picture at the head of the advertising column. It must have been a terribly slow day for news in the ad game. Three-quarters of the text was devoted to our little upstart agency in Richmond, Virginia. What a coup to be featured in the Gray Lady herself where the presidents and ad managers of companies all over the United States would see us. Practically any ad agency owner would have given up his first born to be in our shoes. Reprints would be run off by the thousand and sent to every prospect from Nova Scotia to Tijuana. My partner would do back flips.

But no. No back flips. He was angry. His name wasn't mentioned. How dare I appear in an article in the *New York Times* and *his* name not be mentioned? He was the creative director, wasn't he? His name was on the door same as mine only ahead of it, wasn't it? He owned *more* stock, didn't he?

Wait a minute. I didn't write the story. Of course I'd talked about my partner in the interview. Sung his praises. The columnist chose not to use that part of what I'd said, that was all. A lot of what I'd said had not made the cut.

This didn't matter. That he was not included was somehow my fault. Not only was this guy even more impossible to live with than usual for the next week or two, I learned later that he actually had pulled our publicist into his office, shut the door, and rather than give her the pat on the back she deserved, threatened to fire her if another story on the agency ever appeared without his name in it.

Needless to say, I was not having fun. It got so bad I started to dread coming in every morning. Perhaps he and I had karma from a former life to work out, I don't know. I wasn't aware of such things then. But in retrospect I believe we would still have some to work out if I hadn't followed the course I did. I had recently learned that one of the things Jesus had told people to do was to love their enemies and pray for them. (See the quotation on pages 56 and 57.) I knew this wouldn't be easy but I thought at least I ought to try. So I decided to pray for this guy. Not for me, for him. I could see the chaos inside. He was like a raw nerve dangling loose and exposed, ready to touch something, anything, and go off like a heat seeking missile. So I prayed. I asked God to bring him comfort and peace. I prayed that this man's splintered soul would be healed and

96

made whole. I asked God to come into his life, to creep into his heart to show him the way to peace and tranquility. Every time I saw him and he upset me, I would pray this prayer the first chance I got.

Something happened I had not expected. I found that these prayers helped *me*. I found that I no longer could feel animosity toward him. I could not harbor the anger I'd felt once I'd prayed for him. It was as though it had been lifted away. The burden was gone. I felt light, buoyant.

This by itself would have been reason enough to have done what I did, but to my astonishment it was not the only good thing that happened. Within two months from the time I started praying for him he called me into his office and announced he was retiring. To say I was surprised would be a gross understatement. He was only 54 and had never even hinted at the possibility.

Doctor's orders, he said. He'd had a heart attack a few years before and a stress test had revealed that blockages recently had formed. They were still at the point where they could be taken care of without high-risk surgery, but his doctor had advised him to get out of the business before it killed him. He had to slow down, take it easy, get away from the stress.

I bought his share of the business. I paid more than I should, but that didn't mater. My working life was a pleasure again. My brother joined me in the business and we were able to build up the agency and sell it. Enough was generated to allow me to try my hand full time at writing, which was something I'd always wanted to do. But the real kicker, the most amazing thing is, my former partner was able to do something he'd always wanted to, which was paint. Fine art was a passion he'd neglected in favor of the ad business and the almighty dollar, so he was able to turn himself to his real purpose and "follow his bliss."

I saw a feature article not long ago in the newspaper and apparently he has become a success in this new career. I imagine the blockages are a thing of the past. He certainly looked healthy. No doubt his stress level is down to about zero as well, which means he was led to the peace and tranquility I had prayed he would find.

The lesson this man taught me is to forgive. You can do this, too, by praying for whomever you feel has wronged you. Pray for what you believe will be of benefit to them. When you do, what seems like a miracle may come. If you do not, if you hold onto ill feelings, whatever animosity you harbor will return to you as surely as a lead ball dropped from a tower will hit the ground.

This need to forgive includes forgiving yourself. I know because, as I wrote in the last chapter, I did things when I was young that I felt very sorry for when I was older. At the time I couldn't forgive myself and asked God to even the score, to put me on a level playing field. I got what I asked for. You'll remember I advised you not to ask for the same.

What should you do? Pray for forgiveness instead. Ask that God's peace creep into your own heart.

I know from experience this can be more difficult to do for yourself than for someone else. If you have done something you truly regret, images of it may haunt you. Nevertheless you must get past it, you must move on if you are to develop and grow spiritually. You must do it or you will be blocked; riddled with doubts.

My purpose in writing this book is to unveil the invisible world and man's purpose in a way that those moving away from skepticism will understand and can accept. My purpose is to share techniques which have helped me get in touch and stay in touch with my higher self. By doing so I've arrived on a path that promises a more fulfilling life than I ever imagined possible. This is what I wish for you, but you won't be able to if you feel that you're unworthy.

How can you get past this? I suggest that you find a group that can help. Become part of a circle of others who are at your stage of spiritual development. You need the support and the prayers and the strength of people who accept you.

In deciding where to look for others on the path to associate with you might consider where you were born and into what family and cultural surroundings. Your higher self selected these things. For this reason it does not seem to me that the right choice for someone born and raised in the Midwest of America, for example, would be to join an order of Buddhist monks.

In the United States you will find churches that range from those headed by Stage One Jim Baker and Jimmy Swaggart types who use Christianity as a cover for their wickedness to those that are made up of congregations for the most part well into Stage Four. (When I was a child my parent's Unitarian Church was comprised mainly of Stage Three skeptics.) Visit several churches. See if any send off vibrations that resonate with yours.

Keep in mind that the media is one-sided in its depiction of Christians because it is run for the most part by Materialists. They delight in showing the Stage Ones with their hands in the pockets of simpletons, and Stage Twos who think everyone else has to believe exactly what they believe or they're going straight to hell. Look for a Stage Four church. It won't be as hard to find as you may think. Consider when you visit that to be a true Christian means to to love your neighbors *and* your enemies, which is exactly what you must do, too, if you want to advance.

It also means that by accepting Jesus as your personal savior you will be forgiven whatever wrongs you have done. Imagine. You can dump all that karma, the entire negative bank balance from lifetimes of errant behavior. Be open and receptive to this idea during your visit. Be open as others explain what Christianity means to them. Consider the possibility that paying your karmic debt was precisely why Jesus was born and allowed himself to be crucified. Think, too, about the symbolism of the ritual of Baptism. It represents a death to sin and rebirth with a clean slate, a rebirth because Jesus has paid your debts. If you believe this, it will be true. Remember, "All things are possible to him who believes."

Here's something else to think about. Being a member of a spiritual brotherhood of some kind also may prove beneficial when the time comes for you to make the transition from the physical to the nonphysical world.

I'm reminded of my mother who told me about the time back in 1918 when at the age of twelve she was put on a train in Arizona on her way to boarding school in Canada. The trip was to take eight days and a number of changes of trains would be required. Her father, a Mason, removed his pin and put it on her, telling her to wear it always where others could see. If she had a problem, someone would help. It worked. She traveled all the way across the United States from the far Southwest to Quebec and many times along the way was helped by total strangers. She had tapped into a brotherhood, had become part of a group. When the time comes for you to make your journey into the next dimension it won't hurt to have your own version of a Masonic pin.

In summary, by whatever means you can, forgive yourself and forgive others. Allow a group of fellow travelers on the path to help you. When this has been accomplished you will have made tremendous progress. As you proceed from this point begin to meditate on other truths which have been revealed. For example, that our attachments to the trappings of the physical world hold us back and bring us back again and again. As you recall, this is where the Buddhists place most of the emphasis. It is why Jesus said that it is as difficult for a rich man to enter the kingdom of God as it is for a camel to pass through the eye of a needle. I don't believe he meant that anything inherently is wrong with being rich. The error comes in being attached to wealth and the desires which arise out of the physical world. These desires sidetrack us. They block us from realizing our true nature as spiritual beings. They prevent us from uniting our egos and our higher selves and in so doing truly living life to its full potential.

Let us assume you now have forgiven yourself and others. How can you identify what else may be holding you back?

You can do so by tuning in to your moment-to-moment stream of consciousness and realizing what makes you worried, anxious, resentful, uptight, afraid, angry, and so on.

James said we should be glad when we face trials, remember? Trials can be opportunities to build strength, self control and perseverance. The emotions they generate can be signals which identify fears and attachments that have you blocked. Try to step outside yourself and identify unsettled emotions, tugs and urges which have become part of our programming.

Later, we will discuss how to get in touch with your higher self and to put your intuition to work. Unsettled emotions are the worst form of interference to accomplishing this. As long as they plague you it will be almost impossible for you to distinguish whether your higher self is communicating to you or if what you sense is some aspect of your ego conjuring up a buried fear.

To deprogram yourself, slow down and consider what triggered a negative emotion. Did your temper flare? Why? Why was it so important things go your way? If you retrace what you felt back to its cause, in most cases you will come to a particular variety of fear. It has been said that only two fears are instinctive: of high places and loud noises. The others were acquired in this life or another. Whatever is acquired can be disposed of.

Fears usually can be grouped under one of six headings: the fear of poverty (or failure), the fear of criticism, of ill health, of the loss of love of someone, of old age, and of death.

I've listed the fear of poverty (failure) first because in many ways it can be the most debilitating and insidious. Traits develop that bring it about. For example, are you a procrastinator? An underlying fear of failure is probably the root cause and can be counted upon to produce that result.

Are you overly cautious? Do you see the negative side of every circumstance or stall for the "right time" before taking action. Do you worry (that things will not work out), have doubts (generally expressed by excuses or apologies about why one probably won't be able to perform), suffer from indecision (which leads to someone else or circumstances making the decision for you)?

Are you indifferent? This generally manifests as laziness or a lack of initiative, enthusiasm or self control.

Step back and listen for internal voices that say "can't" or "don't" or "won't" or "too risky" or "why bother?"

How do you get rid of them? Shoo them away.

Whether you are the president of a nation or a company, or a bum on skid row, the only thing over which you have absolute control is your thoughts.

You may say, I can't control what thoughts pop into my head. True. You may not control which thoughts arise but you can decide whether to discard one or to keep it. You can decide that it is counterproductive and throw it away, or you can turn it over and over in your mind, nurture it and let it grow. Whatever thoughts you keep will expand and eventually manifest.

Beginning now, each time you catch yourself with a negative thought, a thought that says "you can't," "it's not possible," "maybe someone else but not me," get rid of it.

But you say, I'm poor, I'm not a good student, I'm not a good salesperson, I'm in the lower third of productivity.

You are what you are because of your thoughts. Your higher self and your unseen teachers and guides all want the best for you but your ego is holding you back because of the way it was programmed.

If what I've been writing about here is a serious problem for you, go out and buy some self-help tapes that will plant positive thoughts in your mind in place of the negative ones. Play them to and from work and before you go to sleep at night. Use self-hypnosis tapes. Play them over and over for at least a month. Get all that junk out of your head and replace it with thoughts that are positive.

What about the other fears? They're to be discarded in the same manner. If you suffer from fear of criticism, for example, it probably came about as a result of a parent or sibling who constantly tore you down to build himself up. You'll know this is a problem if you are overly worried about what others will think, if you lack poise, are self-consciousness or extravagant. (Why extravagant? Because of the voice which says you need to keep up with the Jones.) You must rid yourself of inner voices that tell you to think even twice about what people will say. You must eliminate them.

Let's think for a minute about the fear of criticism.

There have been places and times in history when what others thought was worth worrying about. My great, great, great, great, great, great, great grandmother, Suzanna Martin, for example, was accused of being a witch and hanged in Salem, Massachusetts, in 1692. She probably looked like one. But her downfall was the stir she caused after her husband died. She was able to run the farm successfully without a man around. Think of the talk. Such a thing wasn't possible, or so they believed, without the use of witchcraft.

Her neighbor's opinions mattered a great deal. They led to an unpleasant and untimely death.

What about today?

In Iraq or Iran one might have to watch out, but this simply is no longer a valid concern in developed countries. What others think or don't think of you or anyone else is their problem. Yet worrying about what they think can cause a great deal of misery, create karma which will have to be worked out and cause interference between you and your higher self that blocks communication.

Can you imagine the pain my friend brought himself and his bride by not calling off the wedding because the invitations already had been mailed? He was worried what people would say or think. He got married to avoid criticism, lived with the woman a year and then went through an unpleasant and expensive divorce.

So much for the fear of criticism. How about the fear of ill health?

To want to get rid of this it should be enough to know that what you worry about happens. Ever noticed that it's the people who talk about illness, worry about illness, are preoccupied with this or that possible illness, think they feel a pain here or there or were exposed to some germ, who are precisely the people who stay sick most of the time? The power of suggestion is at work.

Suppose you're a tennis buff. Next time you're in a big match and it's close and you arrive at a crucial point and your opponent is serving, holler out, "You're playing great today, Morris. Don't blow it. This is a big point coming up. Try not to double fault." You've started him worrying.

103

Watch him double fault. It's dirty. It will create negative karma. But it works.

How about the fear of the loss of love? This one manifests itself in the form of jealousy and is self-fulfilling like the others. The person you try so hard to hang onto feels smothered and you end up pushing them away. Try being yourself instead. Give them room. It they leave you, they would have done so anyway. You need to develop a sense of worth that isn't dependent on a relationship with someone else.

Next is the fear of old age. This is closely connected to the fear of ill health and the fear of poverty because these are the conditions a person really is concerned about deep down. The power of suggestion is hard at work here, too. If you think you're too old to do this or that, you will indeed be too old.

Consider this. My one-year-old daughter is the same flesh and blood as my wife and me. I saw her when she was born, still connected by an umbilical cord. My wife was just over thirty and I was almost fifty. Yet the cells in my body and in my wife's body and in my daughter's body all were the most recent in an unbroken chain of division that dates back to the first life on earth, all approximately the same age. Billions of years. Why should I be the one who is old? (As far as I'm concerned I'm not, and people tell me I look at least 10 years younger than my chronological age.)

Your physical body is the overcoat of your astral and mental bodies. It gets old and decrepit because you expect it to. (Sure, there might be some enzyme involved, but it's your thoughts that trigger its release.) You aren't aware of your astral and mental bodies and they don't get old.

Why should any body get old? When you've learned all you can from this life, the time will come for you to check out. This is what you will do. No one says you have to be old. Read *Ageless Body, Timeless Mind* by Deepak Chopra. The bottom line is, it's all in your head. You're not old unless you think so.

Now we've come to that final bugaboo, the fear of death. As you now have seen there is nothing to fear. Consider the millions who have had near death experiences and are no longer afraid to die. They're convinced they'll be greeted by loved ones who have gone before and by their guides. They look forward to being bathed once again in the all-encompassing light which many have described as total, unconditional love. Most do not expect to experience pain. It has been reported by many that the spirit exits the body the instant it looks as though death is inevitable.

Only a handful who have had hell-like experiences are worried about what they may encounter in the nonphysical world. These folks need to know what already has been made clear to you. Each of us creates his own reality. We experience what we expect to experience, what we think we deserve. In the physical world this takes time. In the nonphysical we create it instantly. If we expect hell, the hell we believe we deserve is the hell we will get. If we expect heaven, our vision of heaven is what we will have.

Anyone who has ever had a lucid dream will understand what I mean. Such a dream is one in which a person realizes he's dreaming. I've had many and I look forward to them because it's more fun than Disney World. As soon as you're aware you're dreaming you can begin to compose the dream, determine the players, the surroundings, the action. Want to fly over the Grand Canyon? All you have to do is "think" this. Fly over is what you will do, no airplane required. (Like anything it takes practice, but I've gotten so I can swoop and turn and loop the loop.)

Want to attend a cocktail party populated by Hollywood stars? That's where you'll be, talking to Robert DeNiro or Jessica Lange. (These characters will, of course, be your own thought projections.)

One goal of this chapter has been to wake you up to the reality that you are a dreamer in the big dream of life and that you can make this dream lucid. Until now you may have thought you were at the mercy of conditions outside yourself, that you've either been lucky or unlucky, that chance has brought you where you are. This isn't true. You've brought yourself to this spot, either consciously or unconsciously. If this is not where you want to be, you've arrived because your ego self was programmed incorrectly.

You're out of touch with your higher self. Perhaps you hear snippets from it every now and then but ignore what it's trying to say because of other voices which beat it back with "can't," "don't," "shouldn't," "too risky." These are the words of your ego. Your higher self wants so much more for you and knows so much more is possible.

Once you wake up you can begin the deprogramming process. After this is complete you'll be in position to bring together your ego self and your higher self to work in harmony. You'll enter Nirvana, the Kingdom of God, know on a gut level the connectedness of all things. You'll determine your surroundings and the outcome of each and every adventure. You'll be a lucid dreamer in the dream of life.

In the next chapter we'll begin to explore how this can be done.

Chapter Five: Reach out and Touch Your Soul

The ego often is considered the enemy of the soul or higher self, but is in fact essential. It creates and maintains our boundaries, our sense of where we end and others begin. Without it we indeed would perceive ourselves as the field, all that is, or God, just as a newborn in his crib may consider himself to be the center of the universe. We must have a clear understanding of ourself as a separate being, however, before a sense of oneness with the field is viable or healthy. Otherwise we may think we are justified in doing exactly as we please, treating the world and others as extensions of ourselves who exist to serve us and to do our bidding.   Narcissism is the term psychologists use to identify the mental condition brought about by the arrested development of the ego. Antisocial behavior is often the result.

A healthy, properly-developed ego on the other hand allows us to open to spiritual development and vision. The ego must grow as we grow so that we become secure in our sense of self. This is the lesson of the previous chapter.

Properly developed, the ego can become the container that can house the soul without threatening mental, emotional, or physical collapse. Without a well-constructed container, however, the journey to the upper level of Stage Four spiritual development is impossible.

Why have so many thoughtful men and women come to the conclusion we must push the ego aside in order to get in touch with our higher selves? They have misunderstood what the ego is all about. Those who possess underdeveloped egos are threatened by contact with the higher self because of buried fears already discussed. An ego's first job is self-preservation. At best, a weak ego is afraid the higher self will get him in trouble; at worst that the higher self will take over completely and swallow or annihilate him.

The primitive ego is also egotistical. It wants to take credit for all the achievements of our higher self and guides, even to the extent of denying the possibility of anything beyond itself. The ego can turn on an individual and bring action to a stop by pushing just the right buttons.

As discussed in the last chapter the simplest way to deal with the underdeveloped ego's campaign of terror is to observe it with detachment. Don't think of the ego as part of you that must be lost for advancement to be made but rather as a part that needs strengthening. Imagine a fearful ego as a child who needs reassurance or as a student who needs to be educated and brought along. This is usually a matter of increasing awareness of where your conscious mind has abdicated control to your unconscious. If you are not where you want to be, it is your unconscious which has taken over and chauffeured you there. Slow down. Put on the brakes. Take the advice of the last chapter. Meditate about your condition. Think about destructive behaviors you repeat. Try to figure out how you got here, and in so doing educate your ego. Strengthen it to the point where you will be able to bring it in touch with your higher self and not have it feel threatened. Otherwise your ego will make a concerted effort to stop the action by drowning out all communication.

The higher self or soul is that part that connects you with the Eternal. It is the individual dreamer who is in contact with the other dreamers and the Big Dreamer, the One Life of which each of us is a facet. It is that part of us which provides a sense of meaning and value. It is what comes through us to create a sense of intimacy with another human being or another creature. The soul or higher self is reaching out to us when we feel the need to know the meaning of life or of our own lives. It is reaching out when we feel a hunger to experience our connection to all that is. It is reaching out when we contemplate our mortality. It is the part of you that led you to this book.

The soul or higher self is most apparent when we are in a period of transition. This may be during one of the seven-year cycles of our maturation, it may be when a child is born, when the death of a friend or loved one occurs, or in the period preceding our own physical death. Many cultures and virtually all spiritual brotherhoods have rituals and myths to aid in and soften these transitions. The lack of rituals and myths, the relative lack of regard for the spiritual dimension in our secular society, can make these passages difficult and lonely.

The techniques which now will be discussed are not meant to take the place of these rituals and myths. The aid and comfort they give can be one of the major benefits of your participation in a circle of others on the path. The techniques that follow are meant to provide you with practical, day-to-day methods for growing closer to your higher self with the ultimate goal of uniting this part of you with your ego to form a true, undivided Self. When this occurs the pot at the end of the rainbow will have been reached. You will experience a sense of wholeness as though you have arrived home at the end of a long journey. Your life will be transformed by a new principle that is in accordance with the order and objectives of the universe. You will be led to a life of abundance, not necessarily of money or possessions, but in the form of the fulfillment and joy of existing in the flow, of leading a life of freedom you did not think possible. You will be aided and guided by unseen hands. You will be in a position to choose because you will sense the outcome before taking action. You will bring the course of your life into harmony with your destiny.

You will have reached the state of enlightenment.

All this sounds very grand and godlike but the truth is, enlightenment is our natural state. It is the state of all creatures in the wild. They are guided by the natural forces of the field. The higher self or the soul of swallows brings them back to Capistrano on the same day every year; it directs the herds of wildebeest across the African plains. It guides the migration of whales.

Man was the same before the mythical Garden of Eden. He remained fully in touch with nature, guided by instincts and higher forces. Or to put it another way, he was at one with God, the Big Dreamer. By becoming self-conscious, however, by becoming aware of himself as separate and apart, he pulled the plug that connected him. What he believed himself to be became his reality. He indeed was separate. He now had free will and was capable of screwing up, and because he was by nature lazy and self-centered he could not help but do so.

Nowadays, you and I and a growing number of our fellow humans are arriving at the end of a long journey. We are nearing the completion of the period in our evolution, both as a species and as individuals, when it was necessary to concentrate our efforts on the development of the ego portion of our psyches. Wild animals such as birds or deer have no egos as such. They are plugged into a state of oneness with others of their species and the field. Our egos, which create and maintain our sense of separateness, have prevented this for all but the most advanced of our species. Until now. Now our goal must be to maintain our separate identities while simultaneously reuniting with our higher selves. When this is done, the last stage of our evolution in the physical world will be accomplished. Our journey on the earth will be complete.

Most of us have been conditioned since birth to discount what is often described as intuition. As a result we've developed a habit of not listening to the voice of our higher self. If we are to reconnect, the first step is to acknowledge that intuition is real, that our higher selves exist, and that it is possible for us to be in touch. This is characterized by a sense of knowing, but not in the ordinary way which requires a subject (you) and an object (what is known). For example, (you) know that (San Francisco won the Super Bowl in 1995). With the intuitive knowledge of the higher self there is no separation of knower and known.

Earlier I wrote about the time I glanced at a door prize ticket and knew instantly I'd won even before the numbers were read. The sensation I had was: *winner.* No subject, no object. This sensation has been labeled Psychic Intuition and was experienced in the area of my solar plexus. It felt as though the string of a viola located inside me had been struck.

Not everyone receives intuitive insights or messages from their higher self or guides in the same way. Some hear voices. For example, after learning I was writing this book, a friend of mine, a founding partner of a large law firm, confided in me about several instances of this he has experienced. One took place between spring and fall semesters of law school when he was at a coming out party at a country club. The debutantes were making their bows, being presented to society as it were, but he was not paying attention. He was standing in a group of friends talking and laughing, much more interested in joking around with them than in the girls dressed in white doing curtsies. Out of the blue a voice said, "Here comes the mother of your children." The tone was like, "Wake up, stupid, and look over there." He wasn't sure whether the voice had come from inside or outside his head and said, "What?" The voice returned with, "The mother of your children is coming." He turned to look. Taking a bow was a young woman he'd met but hardly knew. He had no plan or desire to get married. He thought this girl was attractive but he had no interest in her at that time. Two years later they walked down the aisle. As the voice had told him, she became the mother of his children.

The reception of extrasensory signals in the form of words, a sound or some from of language is called Psychic Hearing. It can be subtle, similar to what one hears in his mind when one talks to himself. It also can be loud and clear the way my friend experienced it.

Another way messages are received is called Psychic

Vision or clairvoyance. This is a form of ESP which expresses itself as a picture, symbol or visual impression. Traditionally, it is associated with receiving visual insights either through meditation or in dreams. You probably are aware of psychics who help police by visualizing the scene of the crime or the location of the body. You may have had experiences with clairvoyance and not realized it. Have you ever had, for example, a mental image of an old friend and then received a phone call or letter from that person?

Psychic Intuition, the instantaneous sense of knowing I experienced when I won the the Sony TV is the most common form of reception. Degrees of this exist, ranging from a fleeting snippet which occurs spontaneously, to a permanent gut-level realization, a sense of knowing that continuously flows. The ultimate state is one in which the receiver "knows" himself to be creation, all-that-is, one and inseparable. I've had glimpses of this. I doubt anyone remains in it long although some practitioners of yoga may approach a continuous state. (I'm reminded of the *New Yorker* cartoon wherein two dapper men in climbing gear are rounding the curve of a mountain pass. One says to the other, "I think I'd better warn you. B.J. has changed some from the old days at J. Walter Thompson." Out of their sight around the bend is a robed and bearded guru-type in the lotus position with thumbs and index fingers pressed together chanting, "Oooommmmm.")

It may take years of working at it, but I believe for most an ongoing connection that gives moment by moment guidance is possible, and a realistic goal. Not that we should discard the rational mind. It has its place. We simply need to recognize its limitations. Our rational mind can be compared to a computer. It can sort the data (anything you have read or experienced), cross tab, analyze and spit out an answer. Unfortunately, no matter how competent your mental computer is the answer may not be correct because the analysis is limited to the data your mind had to work with. This is not to say it isn't of value. It is probably all we need to make the right decisions 90 percent of the time. It tells us red light means stop, green light means go, don't touch a hot stove, one and one makes two, don't spit into the wind, or lick a frozen metal flag pole. A quick scan of one's data base is enough. But your higher self should be consulted on the big issues because it isn't limited in any way. It is plugged into the infinite knowledge of the universe. It has direct access to the dream and the Big Dreamer.

Let's talk about how to cultivate a relationship. Like any, it needs to begin with trust. As we've seen, the ego is terrified of losing control. Yet, your ego must feel confident enough to allow your higher self to come through. To do this I've convinced myself (my ego) that I do not have control, anyway, and cannot have control no matter how hard I try. Nothing is in my control except my thoughts. To believe otherwise is self-delusion. (Once I read that anything one feels he must control, in reality controls him. The twang of the viola vibrated in my mid section. Take this truth to heart and you're on your way.)

Start slow and ease into it. You might begin by setting aside a few minutes each day simply to daydream. Call this your quiet time. Dedicate up to a half hour once or twice a day from now on. It can be the most productive and important period you spend.

Sit back and relax or lie down. Allow yourself to enter a state of consciousness that's different from what you're used to during normal waking hours. You might get a tape or two on meditation to help you relax, but for the first week or so don't meditate. Daydream. This may be enough by itself to create the conditions for insights to come through. Think of a quiet place, perhaps somewhere out in nature, where the temperature is perfect. Perhaps there's a blue sky and a gentle breeze. Allow yourself to go into a kind of trance, to drop to a deeper level of consciousness. Let your mind go wherever it takes you.

You may find that you begin identifying your true purpose and mission in life. Daydreams often are fantasies about who we really are or what we can be. They may be closer to the truth than what you thought was the truth until now.

Ask yourself what you would do if you could expand to your full potential? What is your bliss? (I'm not talking about your ego desire to sit on the beach and play gin rummy, I'm talking about how you would like to be involved in life, not watch it mosey by.)

Some people have a regular quiet time and don't even realize it. This is when they exercise or jog. For me it is a walk I take either in the morning before or in the evening after I write.

No matter when or how you elect to spend time getting in touch, ask yourself, how do your fantasies connect with the circumstances into which you were born? What games did you play as a child? How did you entertain yourself? Have you any interests that go back as long as you can remember?

Are you now doing what you like? Does what you do help others in some way? With your background and training what could you do? If you could have whatever you want, be whatever you want, what is it? How would this help others?

Do this each day for several days. What themes recur? Write them down. A pattern will emerge. Keep at it. Develop this into a vision. Whatever this entails at first may seem impossible, but this may be your ego talking. Don't let it get in the way just because it's terrified. Stroke it. Tell it you're not going to quit your day job. Not this week, anyway. You may modify your vision as you proceed but don't start out by watering it down because of the seemingly "practical" voice of your ego. Your higher self already has the end result in mind. Let it help you bring this into focus.

The higher self also knows how your vision can be achieved. Allow yourself to be shown the way. Ask for guidance in your daily quiet time. Sometimes the information you need will come immediately. Often it will not. Be patient, an answer is on the way. It may arrive in several days or even a week later.

In general women are able to get in touch with their higher self or intuition more readily than men. (This is the source of the "wives tale" of woman's intuition.) The reason is, in our culture women usually are in closer touch with their emotions, and intuition is a kind of emotion or "feeling." Feeling what emotions are communicating is one way to "listen." It also may be that women are more receptive by nature, but no doubt many men have been programmed from birth to deny emotions. The strong silent type was long the role model to which a man was to aspire. Men should not become discouraged. Everyone, male or female, has a masculine and a feminine side. We men may have to work harder, but everyone can feel emotions. It may take longer for us to "receive" an answer, but we can do it guys. Believe me. If I can, you can.

Often I'll ask a question of my higher self and guides at night before I go to sleep. If possible, I phrase the question so that a yes or no answer is sufficient. I conclude by saying, "When I wake up tomorrow, let me realize the best course. Give me a sense of knowing." This almost always works.

You may be wondering, how can I tell if my higher self is telling me something or if it's some other part of me? Many different feelings and conflicts are going on within me at any given time.

In the last chapter we discussed how to identify the flak thrown up by your ego. This revolves around worry and is usually fear based. Disregard it. It has nothing to do with your higher self. Your higher self is never worried; does not know the meaning of fear. Nor is it the part of you that judges or says you must follow the rules. Communication from the higher self has a lightness to it, a sense of "this is right." It is not an addictive voice, either, one that says you need alcohol or drugs or some other person or a new car or a mink coat to make you happy. It is not the one that says, "If only I could get a promotion or win the lottery or score a touchdown then I'd have what I need."

If it has a sense of urgency to it, it probably has to do with some earth-bound fear or addiction. When you are bombarded with this kind of interference, release it. Let it float away. Go under this flak. Messages from your higher self have to do with what is right in the long run. If you ask for the answer to a short-term problem, you'll get an answer that will serve the long haul. You may not understand at the time why you are led in a given way, but when you look back you will. You'll see it had to do with inner things, with what is of true value, not with what will remain forever on the physical plane.

Being guided daily by my higher self has become a way of life, but is not something I expect most will be willing to plunge into. Nor do you need to. Ease into it a day at a time. Try making minor decisions to test how it feels. For example, suppose you go to a party and a feeling says this is not where you want to be. Your ego may counter with, "You can't leave. What would people think?"

Leave. Go home or wherever your inner voice directs you. When you get there, calm yourself. Check your feelings. If you were following higher guidance you'll feel light, more alive. You'll have energy. Learn to recognize this feeling. In the future, even after you've made a big, potentially life-changing decision, you'll experience this same sense of buoyancy if you're following your higher self. If you are not, you'll feel drained, blocked, maybe even depressed, and it's time to reconsider.

As you work at listening to and practice following these messages, you'll find they get stronger and that it's becoming easier to sort out ego-based voices and communication from a higher source. Start with matters that aren't all that important and let your confidence build. If you persevere, you will come to a point where you are willing to let your life be guided in this way.

I won't try to tell you this whole business isn't scary at first. But once you start down this path you won't want to turn back. You'll experience a new sense of freedom. I guarantee it will be an adventure.

Perhaps right now, today, you feel a sense of frustration with your life. You know something's wrong, that you'd be happier doing something else, but you don't know what. Begin consulting with your higher self and asking to be shown the way and you can be confident things will change. There can be no other result. Your ego self will be terrified. Tell it to hang on and trust. Your higher self is a gung ho type who knows no fear.

Ask for awareness, a sense of knowing what you should do next. You might ask at night as I often do, or during your daily quiet time. You may receive an image, a feeling, or an answer in words right on the spot. You may draw a blank. If so, go about your business but expect an answer. Trust that it's on its way. It may come in a dream. It might come from outside yourself. You are part of one big dream, remember? The answer can come from anywhere. Be attentive.

Answers that come from outside me usually arrive in written form. A phrase or paragraph in a book I'm reading will seem to stand out. The medium could be almost anything: A fortune cookie, a comic strip, the Bible, Dear Abby. Whatever it is will strike a cord and have meaning for me and my situation the author probably did not have in mind.

How does this work for me on a day-to-day basis? If a question or problem occurs in the morning while I'm working, when lunch comes I'll check my feelings to see if a trip to the library or a bookstore seems indicated. If so, I'll walk in and go to whatever section or shelf feels right, take a book from the shelf and open it at random. More often than not the answer will be on that page. If not, I'll flip a few pages and look again. If the answer isn't there, I'll try another book. Seldom do I pick up more than three. Many of the quotations used in this book were uncovered this way.

A friend tells me his answers usually come from other people. It could be something the preacher says in a sermon on Sunday. Or my friend might be engaged in a conversation at work about something totally unrelated and a sentence or phrase a person says will jump out at him. He has his answer. The meaning for him may have nothing to do with what was being said.

Ask your higher self to direct you to a better life. Let it show you step by step. Don't try to force it. Don't make yourself make decisions. Just let things take place. If you allow yourself to be guided, things will happen. Remain flexible. Trust. Things probably will not occur the way you expect, nor will you end up where you thought at the outset your higher self was taking you. If you go down a path only to find a dead end, look around for the open door. You will find it. You were led down that path because that's where the door is.

Your higher self knows what it's doing. It won't let you starve. At times things may look bleak, though, so be prepared. For example, you may wonder what's taking so long. Your higher self and guides seem to delight in cutting things close. Their scheduling often seems just in the nick of time.

Something that at first seems a disaster may happen. You might lose your job. If so, it will be part of the plan. A much better opportunity will come along.

Let me give you an example from when I was doing my best to build up the ad agency I wrote about earlier. The National Rural Electric Cooperative Association account went into review. It seemed ready made since my staff and I had considerable experience in the electric utility field. It was a million dollar account, not huge but not small, and it was located in Washington, D.C., only a two-hour drive from our offices. The people at NRECA were friendly and seemed to like us. The fit looked perfect on paper. Nevertheless, something told me the account was not right for us. At the time I was still listening to my ego fears, to the "shoulds" and "shouldn'ts" and "don't be sillys." The latter rang loud and clear, so we pressed ahead. We needed the business. What could possibly be wrong? This was a national account with an excellent credit rating. The people were fun to work with. They liked us. We liked them. Damn the torpedoes.

The sense that something wasn't right continued nagging me, but my ego assured me we'd win the business. This part of me was so hopeful I allowed my company to invest inordinate manpower and to make out of pocket expenditures on a trial project that would take years to recoup. I told myself we needed to make the investment and was assuaged because during the process we became quite friendly with the advertising staff. Before long they were sending all the right signals. I was practically counting the money we would soon be making to earn back our outlay when the ad manager paid a personal visit. Over a very expensive lunch (which she paid for) she told me our agency would not be awarded the account. A higher up in the organization we hadn't met had overruled her wishes and the wishes of her staff. The business would go to an agency in Baltimore.

Part of me was devastated. Part of me said, "I told you so." But my intuition being dead right isn't the kicker. Two months later the Virginia Power account went into review. This was a $5 million client located in our hometown. We landed it with relative ease. No travel would be required and it was five times the income! If we had landed the association of electric cooperatives we'd have been precluded from competing for the business. Virginia Power is an invester-owned utility. NRECA is an association of user-owned utilities. The philosophies and goals of these two organizations are diametrically opposed. It would have been like having the RC Cola account when Coca-Cola went into review, a bird in the hand when the one in the bush is many times as large.

When we ignore our intuition we are not always as fortunate as I was on this occasion. What had looked like a disaster turned out to be an act of grace. Even so, if I'd listened to my intuition I'd have saved my company a great deal of money and the people who worked so hard to win the business a lot of heartache. The message is to follow your intuition even if you don't understand why it's telling you what it is. Trust and persevere. Trust that in the end you will be better off. Persevere until you find the open door.

The question is bound to arise, can your higher self make a mistake? Can it lead you down the metaphorical primrose path? The answer is an emphatic "no," it cannot make a mistake. You may make a mistake interpreting it, but your higher self and guides know what they're doing. They're plugged into the big dream and in constant touch with the Big Dreamer.

Be cautious. Be cautious until you are one hundred percent confident in your ability to understand what you are being told. Ask for confirmation. Ask for reassurance. Ask and you will receive. But do not ignore your intuition. If you do not pay attention to it, if you do not move at least cautiously in the direction it is pushing you, you'll become blocked. Listening to your higher guidance and learning to understand is like any skill. The more you do it, the better you get at it and the easier it becomes. Like anything, use it or lose it. If you happen to make a wrong turn, the mistake will not be a disaster if you honestly were trying to do the right thing. Your guides and your higher self will come to your aid in such situations.

Write down your fears. Turn these statements around into positive affirmations. "My needs are being taken care of." "My life is getting better and better." Repeat them to yourself whenever the negative thought reoccurs. And keep in mind what Jesus said:

> And do not set your heart on what
> you will eat or drink; do not worry
> about it. For the pagan world runs
> after such things, and your Father
> knows that you need them. But seek
> his kingdom, and these things will
> be given to you as well.

Luke 12:29-31

It helps to have at least one other person you can talk to about your fears. This should be someone who is also following the path laid down by their higher self. It should not be a family member, co-worker, or anyone who is still in the skeptical Stage Three mode. They only will reflect your ego fears.

And pray. Pray for guidance. Pray for the best possible outcome in each situation. The power of prayer is very real as we will see in the next chapter.

Chapter Six: Prayer and Grace

One would not know it from reading or viewing Materialist owned and operated media, but the efficacy of prayer has been demonstrated in scientifically constructed experiments. One example of such a study is that of Randolph Byrd, a cardiologist, who over a ten-month period used a computer to assign 393 patients admitted to the coronary care unit at San Francisco General Hospital either to a group that was prayed for by home prayer groups (192 patients) or to a group that was not prayed for (201). This was a double blind test. Neither the patients, doctors, nor the nurses knew which group the patients were in. Roman Catholic as well as Protestant groups around the country were given the names, something of the condition of their patients and were asked to pray every day, but were not told how.

The patients who were remembered in prayer had remarkably different and better experiences than the others. They were three times less likely to develop pulmonary edema, a condition in which the lungs fill with fluid; they were five times less likely to require antibiotics. None required endotracheal intubation (an artificial airway inserted in the throat), while twelve in the un-prayed-for required this. Also, fewer pray-for patients died, although the difference between groups was not large enough to be considered statistically significant.[1] If this had been a new drug or medical procedure being tested and these results were achieved, headlines would have been blasted across medical journal covers and the health pages of newspapers.

Physical distance from the patient was not a factor in the results achieved. It did not matter whether a prayer group was located in the same town or across the country. This will come as no surprise to those familiar with quantum mechanics if they will think of prayer as information as opposed to energy. The intensity of energy diminishes as the distance it travels increases, and its speed is limited to that of light. As we learned in Chapter One, however, information is transmitted instantaneously anywhere within the field. Distance not being a factor is also seen by those who have had the sensation of knowing that a loved one or relative located halfway around the world has been killed, injured, or is in danger. Those who have experienced out of body travel also say all that's required to be in the presence of a particular person or in a given place is to think about that person or place.[2] Our thoughts are transmitted anywhere, instantly. Such is the nature of the field.

An organization exists which has as its purpose the study of how prayer works and techniques that produce the best results. It was founded by Christian Science practitioners who have been at this since 1975. (It is called Spindrift, Inc., and the address is: P. O. Box 452471, Ft. Lauderdale, Florida 33345.) Resting next to my keyboard at this moment is a document an inch thick, printed on both sides of 8-1/2 by 11 paper which set me back $29. Called "The Spindrift Papers," it gives detailed information of experiments conducted under rigorously controlled conditions, the highlights of which I will now share with you for the price of this book.

The first question Spindrift researchers sought to answer is, does prayer work? The answer as we already know is yes. In one test rye seeds were split into groupings of equal number and placed in a shallow container on a soil-like substance called vermiculite. (For city dwellers, this is commonly used by gardeners.) A string was drawn across the middle to indicate that the seeds were divided into side A and side B. Side A was prayed for. Side B was not. A statistically greater number of rye shoots emerged from side A than from side B. Variations of this experiment were devised and conducted but not until this one was repeated by many different Christian Science prayer practitioners with consistent results.

Next, salt was added to the water supply. Different batches of rye seeds received doses of salt ranging from one teaspoon per eight cups of water to four teaspoons per eight cups. Doses were stepped up in increments of one-half teaspoon per batch.

A total of 2.3 percent more seeds sprouted on the prayed-for side of the first batch (one teaspoon per eight cups of water) than on the unprayed-for side (800 "prayed-for" seeds sprouted out of 2,000 versus 778 sprouts out of 2000 in the not-prayed-for side). As the dosage of salt was increased the total number of seeds sprouting decreased, but the number of seeds which sprouted on the prayed-for sides compared to the unprayed-for sides increased in proportion to the salt (i.e., stress). In the 1.5 teaspoon batch the increase was 3.3 percent. In the 2.0 teaspoon batch, 13.8 percent. In the 2.5 batch, 16.5 percent. In the 3.0, 30.8 percent. Five times as many prayed-for seeds in the 3.5 batch sprouted (although the total number which sprouted was small as can be seen from the chart below). Finally, no seeds sprouted in the 4.0 teaspoon per eight cup batch.

Salt	Control / Grown		Prayed-for / Grown		% Increase[3]
1.0	2,000	778	2,000	800	2.3
1.5	3,000	302	3,000	312	3.3
2.0	3,000	217	3,000	247	13.8
2.5	3,000	454	3,000	528	16.3
3.0	3,000	52	3,000	68	30.8
3.5	2,000	2	2,000	10	400.0
4.0	3,000	0	3,000	0	0.0

What this says is what people in foxholes and other tight spots always have known: the more dire the situation, the more helpful prayer will be. Up to a point. (There comes a time when things are so bad nothing helps.)

The experiment above was also conducted using mung beans. The solution of salt and water ranged from 7.5 teaspoons per eight cups of water to 30.0 teaspoons per eight cups. The increase in the number of sprouts for the prayed-for side ranged from 3.3 percent to 54.2 percent.[4]

Next an experiment was constructed to determine whether the amount of prayer makes a difference. This involved soy beans in four containers. One was marked "control" and not prayed for. The other three were marked X, Y, and Z. In each run of the experiment the X and Y containers were prayed for as a unit and the Y and Z containers as a unit. So, Y received twice as much prayer as either X or Z. The Y container also had twice as many soy beans germinate. The results were in proportion to the amount of prayer.[5]

This is reminiscent of a principle set forth by Napoleon Hill in his perennial bestseller, *Think and Grow Rich*. He wrote this grand daddy of all self help books in the 1930s and updated it in 1960. One chapter is devoted to the principle he called "The Master Mind." Hill suggested that whatever project or purpose or goal an individual had it could be advanced and achieved most readily by bringing together a group of people who could apply their unified brain power to it. Hill never used the word prayer nor did he suggest people sit around and pray. But he did liken a group of minds at work on a project to a group of storage batteries connected together in a series to produce much more power than any single battery possibly could on its own. He wrote, "When a group of individual brains are coordinated and function in harmony, the increased energy created through that alliance becomes available to every individual brain in the group."[6] He cited several examples including the remarkable successes of Henry Ford and Andrew Carnegie each of whom had a group of colleagues around him working and pulling together on common goals.

Hill wasn't referring only to innovative thinking that leads to marketing and sales results. He was talking about much more, of an aura being created which leads to favorable events taking place, or to what might be considered by Materialists as "good breaks." The Master Mind creates a force with a life of its own, a force I've called Grace later in this chapter. It works like unseen hands. A case Hill cited was that of Mahatma Gandhi who led the successful non-violent revolution that freed India from British Colonial rule. Hill wrote, "He came to power through inducing over two hundred million people to coordinate, with mind and body, in a spirit of harmony, for a definite purpose."[7]

If one person can make 54.2 percent more saltwater-soaked mung beans sprout through the power of his mind, imagine what two hundred million can do. They toppled a government which had been in power for over 150 years and did it without firing a shot.

The power of the Master Mind is another reason I suggested you become part of some sort of spiritual brotherhood. You may want to organize a study group as well. I propose it range in size from three to ten and that it be dedicated to the expanded consciousness and spiritual growth of each of its members. It ought to meet a minimum of twice a month and more frequently if possible. I participate in three such groups and have experienced quantum leaps in my own development as a result.

The group ought to study a text such as this one, another like it or the Bible or the Bhagavad-Gita. Share your thoughts, your individual interpretations of what you study, and ideas about how to put what you've learned to use. You'll also want to set aside a time at each meeting to share personal concerns, fears and troubles. Prayer is one of the tools your group can employ.

Is there anything else the Spindrift researchers learned which would be helpful to know?

The quality of prayer is a factor as well as the quantity. Like anything, practice makes perfect. More experienced practitioners got better results than less experienced practitioners. Get in the habit of praying. Do not save it only for times bullets are flying overhead or the airplane you're on goes into a tail spin.

The Spindrift research also gives us clues on how to pray. First, you need to know what you're praying for. Some experiments were conducted in which the prayer practitioner was kept in the dark about the nature of the seeds he was praying for. He or she did not know what kind of seeds they were or to what extent they may have been stressed. Results showed a drastic reduction in the effect of prayer. The researchers concluded that the more clearly one is aware of the subject, the greater the effect of his prayers will be.

Another experiment measured the efficacy of "directed" versus "nondirected" prayer. Directed prayer was that in which the practitioner had a specific goal, image, or outcome in mind. He attempted to steer the seeds in a particular direction. A parallel in healing might be for blood clots to dissolve or for cancer to isolate itself in a particular place in the body (where it can be cut out). (In the seed germination experiments it was praying for a more rapid germination rate.) Nondirected prayer used an open-ended approach in which no specific outcome was held in the imagination. The person praying did not attempt to imagine or project a specific result but rather to ask for whatever was best for the seeds in an open-ended spirit of "Thy will be done." Both approaches worked, but the nondirected approach was more effective, in some cases producing twice the results.

This is bound to conflict with the beliefs of many who hold that one must visualize a specific result, hold it in his mind and will it to come about. No doubt in some cases this does work. But from what we've learned in the course of this book, the nondirected approach indeed makes more sense. The theory put forth by Spindrift researchers is that prayer reinforces the tendency of an organism which is out of balance to return to balance. The goal of nature is harmony and prayer supports this. To quote the research document, "If the power of holy prayer does, indeed, heal, then such a power will be manifest as movement of a system toward its norms since healing can be defined as movement toward the optimal or 'best' conditions of form and function."[8]   (They did not try experiments in which prayer was used to try to prevent seeds from germinating. If they had, and if what they said here is true, this would not have worked.)

With our limited knowledge we cannot know the best way for an organism to achieve balance. Likewise, the higher self and the Big Dreamer are interested in the growth and evolution of your soul and mine. This seems to correlate. They are looking for harmony and balance, for healing of the soul. With our limited knowledge we cannot know the best way to achieve this. If a new Mercedes will not help foster your spiritual development or someone else's in some way, you're wasting your time praying for it no matter how clearly you can picture just such a shiny new auto in your mind. Consider what James, the brother of Jesus said. "You do not have, because you do not ask God. When you ask, you do not receive, because you ask with wrong motives, that you may spend what you get on your pleasures." (James 4:2-3.) Our motives need to be in line with the goals of the universe. God is not in the business of satisfying our selfish whims. He wants something much more valuable. He wants our souls to heal.

How can we presume to know what is best for stressed seeds or even for our own growth when our conscious minds are working with only a small fraction of the data? Our higher selves are in touch with the Big Dreamer and the big dream; in touch with the field where all the information can be found. The way to the best result may be exactly the opposite of what we expect.

Take the case of Dr. Weiss and his wife and the infant son born with a heart defect. (Chapter Three, page 88.) I do not know whether they prayed about this, or if so what they prayed, but if they did, the natural inclination would have been to pray for the baby to be cured. Being a physician, Dr. Weiss even may have tried to visualize how this could come about. But his prayers would have gone unanswered. He and his wife would not have understood why; perhaps they would have become angry with God or alienated from their faith. They would have had no way of knowing their infant son was in reality a friend from another life who was making a tremendous sacrifice so a karmic debt would be paid and Dr. and Mrs. Weiss would have an experience which would foster their spiritual growth.

Rather than pray, "Please cure my baby," they'd have been wiser to pray for the best outcome for their baby and thereby put the situation in infinitely more intelligent hands. In this case the best outcome for the child would have been a swift and painless death.

It may be irreverent, but I'm reminded of a country music song. After seeing the now fat and ugly high school sweetheart he so dearly wanted to marry many years before, the singer thanks God fervently for unanswered prayers. The universe always knows what's best in any given circumstance.

When our specific prayers are answered it is done in a way that aids our spiritual growth whether or not we had spiritual growth in mind. What we experience may also cause us to consider being less specific next time. You'll recall my prayer to have events take place that would wipe out the bad karma I felt was hanging over me. The experience allowed me to grow a great deal. Even my wife divorcing me turned out for the best as such things always do. Neither of us had been happy for some time. Both of us are remarried now and more content than we have ever been.

A friend in one of my study groups recounted a story recently about how we should watch out what we ask for. Her son had spent a miserable autumn and winter, first on the bench of his high school football team and then on the bench of the basketball squad. Lacrosse season was getting underway and the first game was scheduled for that afternoon. Her son was in the starting lineup. At last he would have a chance to show his prowess. "Please, Lord, have him score a lot of goals," she prayed. "Let him be the star of the team today."

She was thrilled and amazed as she watched the game. Not only did his team beat its opponent, her son scored all the goals for his side. He was all over the place; seemed to be everywhere at once. She patted herself on the back and praised the Lord all the way home. But her joy was short-lived. When her son came home he was depressed.

"What's wrong?" she asked. "You should be feeling good about yourself. You were sensational today."

"Aw, Mom. No I wasn't. I was a ball hog. It was like I never gave anyone else on my team a chance. It didn't even feel like it was me out there playing. It was as though I was possessed. Like someone else scored those goals."

My friend had wanted a feel-good experience for her son and herself. What was received was a growth experience for her son and a learning experience for her.

Next time you pray think about what you are really asking. Will it help you or someone else grow? Think, too, about what is happening in the unseen world as a result. Here is what Betty Eadie experienced when out of her body while clinically dead. In *Embraced by the Light* she wrote:

> I saw many lights shooting up from the earth like beacons. Some were very broad and charged into heaven like broad laser beams. Others resembled the illumination of small pen lights, and some were mere sparks. I was surprised as I was told that these beams of power were the prayers of people on earth.
>
> I saw angels rushing to answer the prayers. They were organized to give as much help as possible. As they worked within this organization, they literally flew from person to person, from prayer to prayer, and were filled with love and joy by their work.[9]

Here's what we need to keep in mind about prayer: 1.) Practice makes perfect, or in other words, experienced prayer practitioners receive the best results. 2.) Quantity is a factor. More prayer brings more. 3.) The more a person or group knows about the subject of their prayers, the better. 4.) Prayers should be kept general in nature. Praying for a specific outcome is less effective than praying for the best outcome. 5.) The purposes of the universe ought to be served by our prayers. This includes spiritual growth and development, the healing of the soul, or in the case of physical healing, the bringing of a stressed body or physical system into harmony or balance.

If you truly want to find your purpose, if you want a fulfilling life and the buoyant feeling of following the path laid out for you, if you want to make progress in this lifetime, if you want to enter the kingdom of God, ask for help. Pray for guidance and assistance in bringing this about. Ask to be shown the way. You will be led to the most exciting adventure you will ever undertake.

Once you ask, expect things to start happening, and be prepared for events to take place you never would have chosen for yourself. At first you may find yourself on a roller coaster ride and wish you could get off. What seems disastrous may take place. You may get transferred. Your wife may ask for a divorce. Your apartment building might burn down. Of course, your experience may be different. You might get a promotion, win the lottery, be offered a dream job out of the blue. I predict the path won't be easy, though. Growth takes effort and growth means change, change that will take place in you. Most people resist that. (It's their ego fighting for what it thinks is survival.) Even if you want to change it won't be easy. You will encounter a number of character-building challenges.

A friend in one of my groups said last week that he'd think twice before he asks for something again. He prayed, "Lord, give me more patience." Soon he found himself in a situation that took every ounce he could muster.

This trying experience achieved precisely what he had requested. He has more patience. Lesser situations than what he went through now will be easy. He'd expected God to hand him more patience on a silver platter, to wave a wand so to speak, but he got what he asked for in the only way it could come. He had to learn it. He'd forgotten that without some pain there can't be gain.

When you ask for change, don't be surprised if some of what occurs is unrelated to the central issues. For example, when I was making the transition from advertising-agency president to full time writer, my car started falling apart. It wasn't an old car, but one thing after another went wrong. I believe now this was an outward sign of inward change taking place in my life. Expect this sort of thing. Trust. Continue asking for guidance. If you think you have an answer but aren't positive, don't do anything precipitous. Ask for confirmation or for some form of reassurance. If you were right in the first place, reassurance or confirmation will come.

And expect to be helped by the invisible hands of Grace. What is Grace? Grace is conditions, events and phenomena which support, nurture, protect or enhance human life and spiritual growth. Grace comes to us from the invisible world and works in all sorts of ways. Just how cannot be explained within the confines of our current body of scientific knowledge. I believe our guides primarily are responsible for the Grace each of us experience. But there are forms of Grace which seem to be universal. Our immune systems, for example, are one form of Grace at work. Modern medicine has only a vague idea why one person who is exposed to an infectious disease will come down with it while another who has experienced the same level of exposure will not. On any given day in practically every public environment the number of potentially lethal microbes and viruses on surfaces or floating in the air is too numerous to count. Yet most people do not get sick. Why? Doctors would say it is because most people's resistance level to disease is fairly high. What do they mean? That most people are not rundown or depressed? Perhaps. But people who are not rundown and depressed sometimes contract infectious diseases.

In some cases, however, getting sick may be an act of Grace. At one point after leaving the ad agency business, I got discouraged. I very nearly threw in the towel on writing full time and returned to the rat race. I took several steps in that direction to the point of having materials printed and putting together a mailing list. It wasn't what I wanted to do, but I was worried I'd never make it as a writer and that my money would run out. So I made a U-turn. Then Grace stepped in. I got sick. I caught the flu. It was a bad case that lasted almost two weeks, and it gave me plenty of time to think.

Whenever I get sick I always ask myself why. Sometimes the answer is that I'm pushing myself too hard and need to slow down. In this case my system was telling me I'd be making a big mistake to reverse my life course. I was as certain of the message then as I am of it now. The viola twanged.

Most people do not get sick and die each day because it is not in the interest of the universe or their higher selves for this to happen. It will not advance their spiritual growth. In my case catching the flu was what needed to happen. It was a wake up call.

The Grace of resistance is not limited to infectious disease. Talk to a state trooper who has been on the scene of many motor vehicle accidents. Ask what percentage of crashes appeared fatal when he first arrived. How many of those actually turned out to be fatal? You are likely to hear some amazing stories of cars or trucks smashed beyond recognition, metal so collapsed, twisted or squashed the trooper will say, "I don't see how anyone could have survived. And yet the person walked away without a scratch," or with only minor injuries. How can metal collapse in such a way as to conform perfectly to the shape of the human body contained inside? Yet I'm willing to bet the trooper will tell you that this happens more often than not.

My one year old daughter has body-surfed down the steep flight of steps from our kitchen to our basement playroom, not once but twice. Another time a babysitter turned her back while changing a diaper. My daughter rolled off a counter top and fell straight to the bare kitchen floor. Any of these three falls easily could have been fatal. None caused so much as a bruise.

Almost everyone has experienced a close call that could have killed him. One day when I was fourteen, I darted across Jefferson Davis Highway without looking. (Why? I was young and stupid.) Before Interstate 95 was constructed this was the main north-south highway on the east coast. This particular stretch had six lanes (three north and three south) with a grass median. I was struck in mid stride by a car in the middle lane. Maybe it was the way the car's bumper caught my foot that lifted into the air, although now that I think about it that doesn't make sense. It seems more logical I'd have been knocked down and run over. Perhaps all seven of my guides got together and lifted me. However it happened, I landed in the grass median. The driver of the car was certain I was dead until I stood and dusted myself off. I didn't have a scratch. The only evidence of the accident was the stain on my trousers where I'd hit the grass and that both my shoes were missing. I found them eighty or a hundred feet away where the car had skidded to a stop. If the laws of Newtonian physics had been working that day I wouldn't be putting this down on paper and the purposes of the universe would have been thwarted. This must be why Grace came to my aid.

Grace is whatever helps advance the evolution of souls. The forms of communication with your higher self discussed in the last chapter fall into this category. The voice telling you to wake up and take notice because the mother of your children is approaching, the clairvoyant message that tells you someone you love is in trouble, a dream that brings the answer to a question. It might be the answer to a prayer.

A friend in one of my study groups and his wife quit their full time jobs to attend seminary together. Now they both work part-time and bring in only enough to get by. Unexpected bills arrived, as they always do. This time they totaled $578, money they simply didn't have. The couple's bank balance registered zero. There was no place to turn. The bills were due. Our group prayed for money to come. No doubt my friend and his wife prayed, too, as well as others.

The couple got an envelope in the mail two days later from the IRS saying their petition had been reviewed and that indeed their tax return from two years back had been found to be in error. Enclosed was a check for $588.

Good timing, you say. True. But the amazing thing is, the couple had not filed a petition or an amended return. Somehow or other, the IRS had made this recalculation on their own. The couple went to their files and checked the return from two years prior. Indeed they found the error which had been referenced.

My experience indicates the IRS is usually not in the mode of helping people out this way. Grace brought them that check. (I'm not sure what the ten extra dollars were for. Maybe breakfast, since our group meets over breakfast on Thursdays.)

This gift of Grace was in accord with the purposes of the universe. The $588 helped further the spiritual growth of this young couple by helping to keep them in seminary.

You may also be familiar with the story of psychiatric pioneer Carl Jung which he related in an article called "On Synchronicity." Jung had a patient, a young woman, who was the type who thought she knew everything. She was well educated and used highly polished rationalism as a weapon to defend herself against Jung's attempts to give her a more human-based understanding of reality. Jung was at a loss as to how to proceed and found himself hoping something unexpected and irrational would happen in order to burst the intellectual bubble she'd sealed herself in.

One day they were in his office, he had his back to the window and she was talking. She'd had a dream the night before in which she'd been given a golden scarab, an expensive piece of jewelry. While she was recounting the dream, Jung heard something behind him tapping at the window. He turned and saw that it was a large flying insect knocking against the pane on the outside, trying to get in. He opened the window and caught the insect. It was a scarabaeid beetle, or rose-chafer (Cetonia aurata), whose golden-green color resembles a gold scarab.

Jung handed the beetle to his patient with the words, "Here is your scarab." This poked the desired hole in her rationalism as Jung had hoped.[10] She had dreamed about the gift of a scarab and now it had happened. What she received, however, was a much bigger gift. She was shown through Grace that everything is one mind, that she was but one dreamer in the dream of life. Grace worked, as always, to aid in spiritual development.

Perhaps you are now saying to yourself, these sorts of things never happen to me. This Martin fellow is living in a fantasy world. To this I will ask, are you making a conscious effort to advance and grow spiritually? If so, are you on the lookout for acts of Grace? You must be open to them and allow them to happen. You must expect them. If Jung hadn't been looking for an unusual, irrational occurrence, if he hadn't been expecting it, he might not have bothered to open the window. If I didn't expect to find a quotation I need or the answer to a question when I walk into a library or bookstore, I doubt I ever would. Suppose it did happen once, even so, and I chalked it up to coincidence? It probably wouldn't happen again. At least I wouldn't see it when it did. You've got to expect Grace to happen and be on the lookout.

Let's suppose you have decided to strike out on the path of spiritual growth. One way to insure you'll be helped along by Grace is to cut off avenues of retreat. This is what the couple in seminary had done. Both had quit their jobs. Perhaps they received help partly because there was no other alternative.

I'm reminded of the general of ancient times who took his army across a sea to fight a distant enemy. As soon as he and his men landed he ordered the ships burned that had brought them. This cut off all means of retreat. It created a big incentive. His men had no choice but to win or die. So they won.

Was it purely the will to live that led to victory? Isn't it also possible they got some breaks as a result of the situation they were in? If you cut off all means of retreat, your guides will be left with no other alternative but to help you. I believe this is precisely what they want to do. They want you to make progress. They want you to wake up and live.

Making the effort to grow spiritually is difficult and it takes courage. By definition growth means change, and most of us think we are just fine the way we are. Our ego self does not want to change for fear that change will wipe it out of existence. This isn't true of course. The new you will be happier, stronger, more vital, alive, awake and aware. But this will take effort. There will be hardships to overcome. Pursuing spiritual growth is not an undertaking for the faint of heart or the lazy.

Human nature by definition means to be lazy. Face

it, all of us are lazy some of the time. Unfortunately, a lot of us are lazy a lot of the time. We think the world owes us a living. We think we can get by without trying all that hard. What we need to get through our heads is that life will be difficult no matter whether we chose to stay put and "play it safe" or to strike out on the adventure of growth. It can either be "life's a bitch and then you die," or "life's a bitch but at least you know why." Stay at it and eventually you'll learn how to live.

Most Christians believe hell is permanent separation from God or Christ. I believe this view and would add that hell also involves separation from one's own soul. (This is the source of the expression, "lost soul.") If you are lazy, if you look only for the easy way, you will end up doing a lot of evil. Not only will you pile up a great deal of negative karma, you run the risk of becoming so separated from your higher self or soul it will be impossible to find your way back. People who are evil are those who have "sold out" to the easy way. They have lost all touch with their souls and may never reunite with them. They may spend eternity looking. This surely is the worst kind of hell.

People who elect the easy way end up spending most of their effort trying desperately to hold themselves together. What a terrible way to go through life. (Or eternity.) If they do decide to spend some effort to improve their existence they may decide an investment of energy in the pursuit of money or success will be the best way to insure the maximum return. But fears of falling apart can never be overcome by money or so-called success. If anything, being way up on top with a big fat mortgage and a lot of "responsibilities" only makes the prospect of falling look even more intimidating. This approach to life becomes an almost unbearable burden because it invariably leads to conditions a person feels he must control through effort and will power in order to keep his life together. Yet, as I've said, anything a person feels he must control, controls him. I've come to the conclusion it is better to let go of all that and submit oneself to one's higher self. Even with the difficulties that surely will come, it will turn out to be the easiest way in the end.

Why not strike out on the path? When you and I differentiated out of the field to become separate and unique entities, each of us cut off any avenue of retreat as surely as the general who burned his ships. If we make no progress in this lifetime, if we do not learn the lessons we are here to learn, we will have to come back and try it again. And again. And again. In between tries we will have to suffer the sorrow that an understanding of the full impact of each of our transgressions will bring as well as the sadness and frustration of knowing what might have been if we hadn't been so lazy or bull-headed. This will be our hell if we are lucky. If we are so lazy that we have actually sold out, we may not even get another chance. We may be doomed to eternal hell and separation. Don't let that happen.

Getting on the right path is what each of us needs to do and what I hope for you. In the next chapter we will assemble what we have learned and lay down a road map to follow.

Chapter Seven: Which Way Will You Go?

In striving to get a handle on my mission in this life I've earnestly tried to think back as far as I can to the very first thing I can remember. Occasionally, I've had glimpses of what I think might be previous lives. One that reoccurs is being in an airplane, a World War II fighter. I'm the pilot. I'm in a tight bank desperately trying to outmaneuver an enemy aircraft that's diving from two o'clock with cannons blazing. (I'm not sure which side I'm on, but I'm either German or American. Not Italian, French, British or Japanese.) My plane is hit. I go into a spin.

To tell the truth I don't know if this is actually a memory or a scene from some long forgotten movie I saw as a child. I was born in 1944 so the timing is right for either.

Once when I was in France I took a flight in a small plane piloted by an old man, a friend of my father-in-law, who offered to turn the controls over to me. He asked if I'd ever flown a plane.

"Never," I said.

"Here. Give it a try."

138

I did. As I had expected it wasn't difficult. From the moment I took the controls I was able to bank and turn.

The old man was amazed. "Go on," he said. "Keep going."

I circled the field we'd taken off from.

"Take her down," he said. "You can do it. Land the plane."

I continued to circle until the runway was directly ahead, then started down. A few hundred feet from touchdown, I lost my nerve and returned the controls to him. But I'm almost certain I could have landed that plane.

He said he'd been flying more than fifty years and had never seen someone who hadn't flown a plane handle one as I had. The vision flashed in my mind of being in the cockpit of that World War II fighter, my hands on the joystick.

I've had other experiences that seem to bring back memories of former lives. There is, for example, a castle in France that gives me a strong sense of déjà vu. Each time I approach, it's as though I'm returning from the Crusades.

Other places in France give off a similar sense of familiarity, but they are not from the same life. They are ancient sites where Druids lived and worked and worshiped.

I was a Druid. I can feel it as surely as I feel eyes on my back. Even though I was born in America, my life unfolded in such a way that I was led to spend a good deal of time in France so that I would remember. My mission of writing this book is a direct result of that life or set of lives in pre-Christian Europe. My guides are friends from that epoch. The last I saw their faces was the moment before I left the causal plane and entered into this physical body. They were dressed in long gray robes, gathered close around me, laughing and joking. It was a kind of farewell party. They were kidding, jostling me, saying, "Don't worry, we'll be with you. Only you won't be able to see us. Not until you return." I have not experienced anything close to it since, bathed as I was in a delightful aura of love so strong it cannot be described. And joy. Such joy. Nothing in life comes close.

I don't remember being born, but I do remember

139

looking up from my crib. I never had the sensation of being the center of the universe that logic says an infant would. I knew I was I, separate and unique, and wondered where my friends were. I possessed no memory but their faces and the feeling of love and joy they gave. Where had they gone? I missed them. I longed to be in the glow of their presence.

At last faces did appear. Disappointment settled in. They were not my friends. I did not know these people whom I later came to realize were my mother and father, brother and sister.

So began this incarnation. I now have come to understand my mission is three fold: 1.) To be a guide to my son and daughter until they no longer need me. 2.) To continue my own evolution. 3.) To explain why you are here and to encourage you to wake up and find your path.

In other lives you knew. Not so long ago, back when we Druids worshiped nature gods and cut mistletoe from the sacred oak tree with a golden knife you looked up at the great arch of night sky, saw a million stars and were filled with a sense of mystery. In the mornings the sun miraculously rose in the east, rays of it shot across the heavens and lit up the underbellies of clouds. You knew in such moments you were one tiny facet of a wondrous creation more astounding than words could convey. You felt communion with all that surrounded you, but unlike all that surrounded you, in some ways you felt separate, apart and distinct. Nevertheless the owl and the deer and the woodland creatures were your cousins. You worshiped them and their spirits and they returned the favor by providing you with the food you ate and the clothes you wore and the covering for your dwelling that kept out rain and snow.

In time, though, you came to understand you were different. These creatures were driven by predictable instincts. The course and timing of their migrations, their habits of reproduction and birth were as predictable as the seasons. As sure to happen on schedule as the summer and winter solstice. The animals had no choice. You could behave as you pleased. You could stay another day, take a different route. Have your babies in the fall, or winter.

Even so, you almost always lived life in accordance with a spirit that guided you with a higher understanding than your own. To do otherwise would have been foolhardy. And if you lost touch, if you were unable to contact the spirit on you own, the Druids could be counted on to do so.

Unconsciously you knew your purpose. It was built into the cycles of the seasons, of spring and summer and fall and winter, of birth and life and death and sleep. And rebirth. It was to grow and evolve. It was to become what you had come from. You would be a new creation by remaining conscious of being separate. It was the way of nature and could be seen in the deer and the rabbit and the bear. You had become separated from the mother of your soul as they had become separated from the mother of their birth. This was the way. You would evolve into a new creation as surely as a seed that fell to earth would grow into a giant oak.

But time went by, incarnations came and went, and you lost sight. You lost the sense of sacredness of all-that-is and you lost touch with your purpose. This was as it had to be. For you to grow and evolve to encompass all and still maintain your own identity, it was essential that your sense of separation become strong. So you began to view the world not as one but as separate pieces, not as a unified whole but as a collection of rocks and trees and individual plants and animals. Even the animals became to you as if they were made of distinct parts such as hearts, eyes, kidneys and bones. You lost all touch with the invisible. You ignored your intuition and the call of the spirit and came to believe the five senses of the physical world provided all that was needed for you to know and understand. Your separation was now utter. You were lost and fell into despair.

This was necessary. You had to lose your soul before you could find it. But the state of being lost is a dangerous place. Now you and others are in jeopardy of eternal separation. If you continue on a path that diverges from your soul you may wander too far. When next you cross over to the nonphysical you may find the way is not clear. You may be misled by entities you mistakenly believe to be benevolent, and they will gain power over you.

Mankind is on a spiritual journey. Like W. E. Butler's flock of sheep we slowly are climbing the mountain. Not all will make it. The oak produces many acorns but only a small number grow into trees. This isn't hard to understand. The way is difficult. It takes courage and it takes a willingness to change. Man hangs onto his self-centeredness. It isn't easy to let go. To grow requires sacrifice and effort, and man is by nature lazy.

But laziness is not the only difficulty which must be overcome. We are surrounded by a culture dominated by the dogma of Materialism, the basic tenet of which is total denial of what cannot be seen or measured by one of the five senses. To combat this, we must keep in mind that one branch of science, quantum physics, denies the very existence of the type of matter necessary to support this view. Quantum physics tells us there is no matter as such, that matter is energy. All that is is one connected whole. There are no separate pieces. What happens here influences what happens there, even if it is halfway across the galaxy. Energy takes time to travel, information is transmitted instantaneously. A slit that is opened changes the field. Observing an experiment affects the outcome.

We are creatures of this nonphysical realm, the nonphysical that supports and informs physical reality. Without the nonphysical nothing on the physical plane could or would exist. The nonphysical is comprised of morphic fields which contain the history of each species. Someday the existence of these fields will be demonstrated scientifically. They contain information which shapes our noses and our feet. And our world. The big field is composed of fields within fields within fields.

Your soul is a morphic field which has been built up over many incarnations. You came from it and will return to it.

For many millennia you existed in the mineral world. You may have followed the evolution of man from the first one-celled animals living in the sea, or perhaps you followed a path through the vegetable kingdom. You were not separate from the field until you realized yourself to be. This happened when you became conscious of yourself during your first incarnation as *Homo Sapiens.*

Then as now you created your own reality. You are who you believe yourself to be in your heart. Just as a tree is known by its fruit, you can know yourself by where you are today. You arrived here through your own actions, whether you took them consciously or unconsciously. You must accept this and take responsibility for yourself if you are to advance.

If you hold love in your heart for yourself and others, love will come back to you. If you hold hate or bitterness, your life will be filled with bitterness or hate. To change your life, you must forgive. You must forgive yourself as well as others.

You came to the physical world to learn these lessons because you needed the thickness of matter to slow down the process of creating your world. In this way you will learn lessons that will remain with you always.

Love is what you must learn. Once you have learned to love perfectly, without selfishness or hesitation, the time for a new creation will be at hand. You will become part of that new creation and continue your evolution. But until you learn to love unselfishly you will continue in the cycle of death and rebirth. If you are fortunate. If you have not gone too far astray.

Your fears block you as surely as bitterness and hate. Therefore you must learn to trust. Once you learn to trust rather than fear, and once you learn to love instead of to hate, the channel between your ego self and your higher self will open wide. This will lead to a new Self who can evolve by quantum leaps. This state is enlightenment.

Life is the dream of God and you are a dreamer within the dream. You have a role or roles to play. You took them on and made a solemn vow to carry them out before you arrived. You can either make good on your promise or you can welsh. The choice is yours. If you welsh you will view the consequences when the time comes for your life to be replayed before your eyes on the second level of the causal plane. You may or may not be given another go at getting it right.

To get started toward accomplishing your purpose you must clear out the junk in the attic of your mind. You must forgive yourself and others. You must get over your fears and replace those fears with faith. You must learn to trust. You must commit yourself to change. You must be willing to suffer hardships and difficulties. You must give up the certainties of the world you have created for yourself until now.

You can begin by devoting a half hour at least once and perhaps twice a day communing with your higher self. When you review your life, think about the decisions you made which brought you where you are. Were they the right decisions? Did you feel good after you made them? Do you like where you are?

You will try to figure out why your higher self chose the circumstances of your birth. You will think back to what you loved to do as a child. You will ask for guidance and you will receive it. You earnestly will follow your bliss.

You will start by following the direction you receive in making small decisions and build up to following it in making the big ones. This will be frightening at first. It will be frightening because you will not know your destination and you will not know how you will get there. But after a while, after you have learned how to trust, not knowing will become part of the fun. It will be like opening packages on Christmas. You will be on an adventure, as thrilling as any attempted by Indiana Jones. You will be the director of your own lucid dream.

Or you may finish reading this book, put it down and forget about it. No doubt this is what many will do. They've spent their lives doing what others told them they ought to. They've carved out a place for themselves. Oh, it isn't all that exciting or fulfilling. And it can be downright difficult sometimes. But they've become quite comfortable with who and what they are. Why change now? There's no proof they're in danger of getting so far away from their higher self they may never find their way back. No conclusive proof can be produced that this nonphysical realm exists. No scientific experiment shows that any part of us survives death. Those people who died and were resuscitated? Like a lot of scientists say, maybe it was all in their heads. It's so much trouble to change. What would people think? Things are comfortable the way they are. Life isn't so bad. Why rock the boat? Plus, this Martin fellow says I can't just change a few little parts of me I know need improvement. He says once I get started I won't want to stop and I may end up changing myself completely. That would be like wanting to remodel the kitchen and calling in an architect.

It's true. Once you get started it will be difficult to stop. The architect will say, "Sure the kitchen needs remodeling but as as long as we're at it, how about a new sun room? Sun room done? Now how about the den? Oh, and you need a wing off to the side. And a second level master bedroom with sky lights and a fireplace."

All the while you're having to live in the middle of this construction, and you say, "Hey wait a minute, I had a nice little bungalow. All I wanted was a remodeled kitchen. You're turning this into a mansion, and in the meantime I have to live with all this sawdust. When will the job be complete?"

The architect will shake his head and say, "Not for a very long time, I'm afraid. You'd better get used to it."

So maybe you don't want a mansion. If this is the way you feel, I doubt there's anything I can say at this point to change your mind. You might as well stick with the bungalow.

I'll tell you something from experience, though. There is no greater joy in life than doing what you are here to do. Getting there will be difficult, it's true. But if you listen and persevere, if you earnestly follow the path laid down before you, you will receive help. Count on it. Look for it. After a while you will begin to sense unseen hands guiding you. The way will become less difficult to find. The trials won't be as hard to bear. There will be blind alleys of course. There will be disappointments of course. There will be tough lessons to learn, but gradually you will come to a gut level understanding of what your existence as a human being is all about. You will come to a gut level

145

understanding of how you fit into the scheme. You will feel at one with it all and yet maintain your separate identity. You will come to know clearly what you are doing. You will sense outcomes before taking action. You will choose which to pursue and which not to pursue. When you arrive at this point you will realize that you have come to power, spiritual power, and with this realization will come joy. Think about it. Whether it's mastery of a sport such as tennis, mastery of the card game of bridge, a musical instrument or a foreign language, the arrival at the state of really knowing what you are doing always brings joy. Imagine the buoyancy that will come with spiritual mastery?

Yet with this joy will come humility. You will be humble because you will know that it is not you who brought you to this state. You will know that it is your guides, your higher self and God. Perhaps there will be some small pride in the knowledge that you finally learned how to listen. But you will be careful to guard yourself against even feeling this because one of the lessons you will have learned on the way is that support is withdrawn from those who think they are accomplishing great things on their own. This is why the saying, "Pride goes before a fall," is true. Be prideful and very soon what you truly can accomplish on your own will be revealed.

There will also come a sense of aloneness. Not loneliness, because you will have friends, you will have family, you will have others on the path. But few if any will have arrived where you have arrived. There will be few with whom you share your feelings and insights, who will understand them completely. If you want a sense of what this will be like, read the Gospels. Time and again you will witness the frustration Jesus experienced because even his closest disciples could not grasp the truth of his words.

Yet, with all this, there will be a new found and deep understanding of your true worth as a human being. How can you understand that Grace exists, how can you know that guides are with you constantly, realize that you have a higher self, sense deep down that you will participate in the building of a new and perfect creation, and all the while continue to think of yourself as meaningless or insignificant?

146

I feel sadness for Materialists and nihilists, which I suppose are inevitably one in the same. If they hold onto the belief that the purpose of life is the mindless duplication of DNA, how meaningless and insignificant they must believe themselves and others to be. What a hopeless state of separation from their souls must be the result. I feel sorry for my parents that it's too late for me or for anyone to demonstrate the error of their thinking. My father died when I was young and my mother is now 88 years old and senile. It's too late for either of them. I can only hope that next go round they will wake up and get back on the path. If they have a next go round.

I feel gladness for you, however, and joy that I might be a conduit in bringing you a deeper understanding of yourself. My sincere wish is that my efforts have helped you move another mile along the journey.

Thank you for taking part of it with me.

Notes

Introduction: Who This Book Is for and Its Objective

1. Butler (1990), page 2.
2. Ibid, page 9.
3. Peck (1993), pages 119-30.
4. Ibid, page 121.
5. Ibid, page 123.
6. Ibid, page 127.
7. Armstrong (1993), page 4.
8. Campbell (with Moyer), (1988).

Chapter One: A New Vision of the Invisible

1. Sheldrake (1991), page 74.
2. Ibid, page 107.
3. Bohm, (1980) page 189.
4. Zukav (1979), page 47.
5. Ibid, page 63.
6. Ibid, page 48.
7. Robinson (1993) page 32.
8. Sheldrake (1991), page 157.
9. Gould (1980), page 181.
10. Sheldrake (1991), page 110
11. Ibid.
12. Ibid, Page 116.
13. Ibid.
14. Sheldrake (1991), page 119.
15. Shepard, (1982), page 117.
16. Danckwerts (1982), pages 380-81.

Chapter Two: The Universe, What and Why?

1. Campbell (with Moyers), (1988), page 207.
2. Johnston (1978), page 32.
3. Campbell (with Moyers), (1988), page 210.
4. Wade (1995), page 20.
5. Watts (1966), pages 14-15.

6. Campbell (with Moyers), (1988), page 211.
7. Gould (1980), page 20.
8. Ibid, page 23.
9. Ibid, page 24.
10. Ibid, pages 20-21.
11. Smith (1986), page 477.
12. Campbell (with Moyers), (1988), page 148.
13. Quoted in Smith (1985), page 143.
14. Campbell (with Moyers), page 162.
15. Smith (1986), page 184.
16.Gibran (1923), pages 29-30.
17. Watts (1966), page 125.
18. Campbell (with Moyers), (1988), page 210.
19. Armstrong (1993), page 81.
20. Ibid, page 83.
21 Alexander (1973 and 1983), page 508.
22. Conner (1994), page G4.
23. Morse (with Paul Perry), page 133.
24. Moody (1988), pages 42.
25. Conner (1994), page G4.
26. Eadie (1992), pages 84-84.
27. Moody (1988), pages 14-15.
28. Eadie (1992), page 58.
29. Ibid, Page 50.
30. Zukav (1989), page 122.
31. Butler (1990), page 8.
32. Ibid, page 98.
33. Campbell (with Moyers) (1988), page 148.
34. Zukav (1989 and 1994), page 245.

Chapter Three: Who Are You?

1. Campbell (with Moyers) (1988), page 229.
2. Kübler-Ross, Pages 64-69.
3. Ibid, page 31.
4. Weiss (1988), page 46.
7. Kübler-Ross, page 15.
8. Ibid, page 172.
9. Weiss (1988), pages 54-56.

Chapter Four: Are You Carrying Excess Baggage?

1. Kübler-Ross, pages 26-27.
2. Allen, James, pages 16-18.

Chapter Six: Prayer and Grace

1. Byrd, Randolph, M.D. (1986), "Cardiologist Studies Effect of Prayer on Patients," *Brain/Mind Bulletin*, page 1, March, 1986. Also, pages 826-829, *Southern Medical Journal* 81:7 July, 1988.
2. Monroe (1985), Page 3.
3. Spindrift Papers, page 1-4
4. Ibid.
5. Ibid, page 1-35.
6. Hill (1960), page 170.
7. Ibid, page 171.
8. Spindrift Papers, page 1051.
9. Eadie (1992), page 103-104.
10. Campbell (1971), pages 511-12.

Bibliography

Alexander, David and Pat (1973 and 1983), *Eerdmans Handbook to the Bible,* William B. Eerdmans Publishing Company, Grand Rapids.

Allen, James (undated), *As a Man Thinketh,* Peter Pauper Press, Mount Vernon, New York.

Anderson, U. S. (1958), *The Secret of Secrets,* Thomas Nelson, & Son, New York.

Armstrong, Karen (1993), *A History of God,* Alfred A. Knopf, Inc., New York.

Bohm, David (1980), *Wholeness and the Implicate Order,* Rutledge & Kegan, London.

Butler, W. E. (1990), *Lords of Light,* Destiny books, Rochester, VT.

Campbell, Joseph with Bill Moyers (1988), *The Power of Myth,* Doubleday, New York.

Campbell, Joseph (1971), *The Portable Jung,* Viking Press, New York.

Chopra, Deepak (1993), *Ageless Body, Timeless Mind,* Harmony Books, Crown, New York.

Conner, Sibella (1994), "The Dark Side of Near Death," Richmond Times-Dispatch, pages G1 and G4, September 4, 1994.

Danckwerts, P. V. (1982) Letter. *New Scientist* 96, 380-81.

Dass, Ram (1978), *Journey of Awakening,* Bantam New Age Books, New York.

Eadie, Betty J. (1992), *Embraced By The Light,* Gold Leaf

Press, Placerville, CA.

Gibran, Kahlil (1923), *The Profit,* Knopf, New York.

Goldberg, Philip (1983), *The Intuitive Edge,* Jeremy P. Tarcher, Inc., Los Angeles.

Gould, Stephen Jay (1980), *The Panda's Thumb,* W. W. Norton & Company, New York.

Herrigel, Eugen (1953), *Zen in the Art of Archery,* Panteon Books, Random House, New York.

Hill, Napoleon (1960), *Think and Grow Rich,* Fawcett Crest, New York.

Howe, Quincy, Jr. (1974), *Reincarnation for the Christian,* The Westminster Press, Philadelphia.

Johnston, William (1978), *The Inner Eye of Love,* Harper & Row, New York.

Karpinski, Gloria D. (1990), *Where Two Worlds Touch,* Ballantine, New York.

Keirsey, David and Marilyn Bates (1978) *Please Understand Me,* Fifth Edition, Prometheus Nemesis book Company, Del Mar, CA.

Keyes, Ken Jr. (1975), *Handbook to Higher Consciousness,* Fifth Edition, Love Line Books, Coos Bay, OR.

Kubler-Ross, Elisabeth (1991), *On Life After Death,* Celestial Arts, Berkeley, CA.

Monroe, Robert A. (1985), *Far Journeys,* Souvenir Press, Ltd., London.

Moody, Raymond A., M. D., (1988), *The Light Beyond,* Bantam, New York.

Morse, Melvin, M.D. (with Paul Perry), (1990), *Closer to the Light,* Ballantine Books, New York.

Murphy, Dr. Joseph (1963), *The Power of Your Subconscious Mind,* Bantam, New York.

Parker, DeWitt H. (1928), *Schopenhauer Selections,* Charles Scribners Sons, New York.

Peck, M. Scott (1978), *The Road Less Traveled,* Simon and Schuster, New York.

Peck, M. Scott (1993), *Further Along The Road Less Traveled,* Simon and Schuster, New York.

Peat, F. David (1991), *The Philosopher's Stone,* Bantam, New York.

Robinson, E. (1983) *The Original Vision: A Study of the Religious Experience of Childhood,* Seabury Press, New York.

Sheely, Gail (1976), *Passages: Predictable Crises of Adult Life,* Dutton, New York.

Sheldrake, Rupert (1991), *The Rebirth of Nature, The Greening of Science and God,* Bantam, New York.

Shepard, Leslie A. (1982), *Encyclopedia of Occultism & Parapsychology Supplement,* Gale Research Company, Detroit.

Smith, Huston (1986), *The Religions of Man,* HarperCollins, New York.

Smith, E. Lester, (1975), *Intelligence Came First,* Theosophical Publishing House, Wheaton, Illinois.

Spindrift Papers, *Exploring Prayer and Healing Through the Experimental Test,* Volume I 1975-1993, Spindrift, Inc., Ft. Lauderdale.

Stevens, Jose and Lena S. Stevens (1988), *Secrets of Shamanism,* Avon Books, New York.

Stevenson, Ian (1974), *Twenty Cases Suggestive of Reincarnation,* University Press of Virginia, Charlottesville.

Wade, Nicholas (1995), "Double Helixes, Chickens and Eggs," New York Times Magazine, January 29, 1995.

Watts, Alan (1966), *The Book,* Vintage Books, Random House, New York.

Weiss, Brian L., M.D. (1988), *Many Lives, Many Masters,* Simon & Schuster, New York.

Zukav, Gary (1979), *The Dancing Wu Li Masters,* Bantam, New York.

Zukav, Gary (1989), *The Seat of the Soul,* Simon & Schuster, New York.

Zukav, Gary (1989 and 1894), *Thoughts from the Seat of the Soul,* Simon & Schuster, New York.

Index

About the Author

Stephen Hawley Martin spent 25 years in the advertising agency business, beginning his career at VanSant Dugdale & Company in Baltimore. He was a principal of The Martin Agency and the founder of Hawley Martin Partners. Clients he has served include: Riggs Bank, Mobil Oil, FMC Corporation, Reynolds Metals, General Motors Corporation, Signet Bank, Virginia Tourism, Lane Furniture, Pet Incorporated, Bassett Furniture, Barnett Banks, USAir, Paramount's Kings Dominion and The Nestlé Company.

In August, 1993, he left advertising to pursue an urge to write. His first novel, *The Search for Nina Fletcher,* was published in 1994 by Books In Motion as an unabridged audio book. (To order call 1-800-752-3199 between 9 am and 5 pm Pacific time.) A second, *The Mystery of Martinique*, will be issued in 1995 by the same publisher. A third, a metaphysical adventure called *Out of Body, Into Mind,* is available from The Oaklea Press.

Stephen lives in Virginia with his wife and preschool children, a son and daughter. His grown daughter attends college in California.

For additional copies of this book, or to order these titles, call 1-800-879-4214:

The Enlightened Companion

A 90 minute audio tape performed by Stephen Hawley Martin. Side one covers key ideas contained in his book, *Beyond Skepticism.* Side two will guide you on a meditation designed to help you overcome buried fears, find your purpose and get in touch with higher guidance. $11.95. ISBN 0-9646601-5-6

Out of Body, Into Mind

Gary Zukav (author of *The Dancing Wu Li Masters* and *The Seat of the Soul)* called this novel, "A delightful adventure." And no wonder. Full of mystery and suspense, it will take you on a roller coaster of a read to a magical island and into the dimension of the mind. You'll visit the lost city of St. Pierre, called by travel writers of the nineteenth century, "The little Paris of the Caribbean." And you'll tour a realm inhabited by the soul. By Stephen Hawley Martin. A quality paperback, 224 pages. $12.95. ISBN 0-9646601-6-4

Under a Lemon Moon

By David N. Martin, this mystery novel reveals true metaphysical insights in a haunting story of murder and revenge that will take you on a spine-tingling karmic journey from Mexico's Sierra Madre mountains to Atlanta's Chattahoochee river . . . and from the valleys of human existence to the heights of uncharted dimensions. A quality paperback, 288 pages. $14.95. ISBN 0-9646601-7-2. Available July, 1995.

The Search for Nina Fletcher

Raised a Virginia aristocrat by a grandmother who kept hidden from her the truth about the mother she never knew, it becomes imperative for Rebecca Fletcher to find her mother when the old matriarch dies or she will lose all hope of keeping the beloved family estate, Live Oaks, from the hands of sinister developers. Swept up by events, she travels to the lovely Mediterranean island of Corsica and into a nonphysical dimension where the truths of human existence are revealed and she learns meaning of her life and that of others. By Stephen Hawley Martin. A quality paperback, 288 pages. $14.95. ISBN 0-9646601-3-X. Available August, 1995.